# IS THE CHURCH IGNORING THE FOUR PS PLACE, PEOPLE, PRAISE, AND PREACHING?

## REVITALIZING CHURCH COMMUNITIES THROUGH FOUNDATIONAL PRINCIPLES

*A Biblical Study Strategy is essential for churches to identify what is missing in their ministries as well as why there is so much attrition.*

Dr. Edmond J. Bergeron

WESTBOW
P R E S S®
A DIVISION OF THOMAS NELSON
& ZONDERVAN

WestBow Press books may be ordered through booksellers or by contacting:

WestBow Press
A Division of Thomas Nelson & Zondervan
1663 Liberty Drive
Bloomington, IN 47403
www.westbowpress.com
844-714-3454

Scripture taken from the New King James Version® Copyright © 1982 by Thomas Nelson. Used by permission. All rights reserved.

Scripture quotations taken from The Holy Bible, New International Version® NIV® Copyright © 1973 1978 1984 2011 by Biblica, Inc. TM. Used by permission. All rights reserved worldwide.

Scripture quotations marked KJV are taken from the King James Version.

ISBN: 979-8-3850-4465-8 (sc)
ISBN: 979-8-3850-4466-5 (hc)
ISBN: 979-8-3850-4464-1 (e)

Library of Congress Control Number: 2025902981

Print information available on the last page.

WestBow Press rev. date: 04/03/2025

# CONTENTS

# ABSTRACT

"Any excuse will do if you're looking for one," a wise man once said. This is a true statement, particularly when it comes to the motivations for church attendance. People in the modern world might readily come up with a wide range of excuses, such as hectic schedules, duties to family, exhaustion, or even discontent with the church itself. Some claim they are not spiritually satisfied, while others may point to issues in their personal lives or their disappointment with organized religion. Others assert, however, that people can worship online or in private just as successfully.

The habit of skipping church has gotten simpler in the era of social media and digital convenience. Many individuals are less motivated to be physically present in a church community because there are so many sermons available online, services can be streamed live, and spiritual information is easily accessible with just a click of a mouse. They think they can satisfy their spiritual demands without ever leaving their homes if they interact with spiritual content, which may be anything from live-streamed services to Bible study podcasts to inspirational posts on social media.

These digital substitutes are convenient and accessible, but they may also be a simple means of avoiding the greater accountability and deeper commitment that come with belonging to a church family. Going to church is about more than just hearing a lecture;

it's about worshiping as a community and as a group. Even while it's a useful tool, social media can never entirely replace the spiritual development and depth of human connection that occur when people gather in the name of their common faith. Consequently, even though there are many justifications for not going to church, the issue still stands: Are these justifications, or are they real?

Creating a warm, interesting, and spiritually enlightening atmosphere is key to drawing and keeping people in church. Building relationships through small groups, mentorship, and fellowship activities encourages people to stay, while outreach initiatives like using social media, organizing community events, and providing pertinent programming help draw people in. Engaging worship, relatable sermons, and opportunities for involvement strengthen members' connection to the church, while pastoral care, spiritual growth opportunities, and inclusivity ensure their needs are met. However, many people may decide to leave if one or more of the "4 Ps"—Place, People, Praise, and Preaching—are absent. These fundamental elements form the cornerstone of creating a church setting that encourages connection, community, and spiritual development.

# DEDICATION

To my wonderful wife, Sherri, who is my best friend, my helpmate, and the person I love most. Furthermore, without your unwavering love, support, and understanding, this book would not have been possible. You are an anointed, God-fearing lady who has been called by God and serves as my sounding board. I will always be grateful for your assistance, which has been my unwavering compass.

My children, Melanie, Jeremiah, Michaela (my daughter-in-law), Carrissa, and Elisha, make me proud and happy every day. Watching each of you grow into remarkable individuals has been one of the greatest blessings of my life.

To Apostle Gregory Hunt, Prophetess Gina Hunt, and their children—Samantha, Gregory, and Angel—thank you for being by my side through every challenge. Your unwavering support, the joy you bring through laughter, and the comfort of your smiles have been a constant source of strength for me.

I am deeply thankful for the prayers, encouragement, and guidance of Apostle Luciano and Pastor Marisol Miranda, as well as the entire community of apostles, prophets, pastors, evangelists, and teachers from International Ministry, Christ His Power in Action Ministries. I will always be grateful to you for your wisdom and lessons, which have greatly influenced my intellectual and spiritual development.

To Strong Tower Church Pastors Jeffrey and Nicola Smith: Your ministry exemplifies what it means to be a community blessing. I appreciate your friendship and example, and your commitment and kindness are admirable.

I want to express my sincere appreciation to my brothers, Joshua, Elliott, and Brian, and their families. I adore you all and treasure the memory of our happy and funny moments spent together. My heart will always have a particular place for those times.

My parents, Paul and Esea, have had an incalculable impact on my life, and for that I am incredibly grateful. You have given me the steadfast conviction that everything is possible if one has faith, trusts in God, and is committed to His will. Dad, I still find inspiration in the scriptures you wrote by hand on the walls of our house. I have read them many times, and they have been deeply ingrained in my spirit, helping me to navigate the difficulties of life. Mom, you have given me strength and inspiration throughout my life with your unwavering love and support. You both gave me values, tenacity, and a strong work ethic, which I cherish greatly. I will always be thankful to you for leaving me a legacy of faith and fortitude. I'm grateful that you helped me become the person I am now.

# ACKNOWLEDGMENTS

To the men and women wearing the uniform of a First Responder and those who are serving, have served, or will serve in the greatest military in the world, the United States of America, I offer my eternal gratitude. Being a former First Responder, I can attest to the role's unwavering dedication, unyielding commitment, and enormous sacrifices, including forgoing the luxuries of ordinary life and being away from family and friends. Your significant work is much valued.

We are grateful to those who keep guard, frequently in the face of extreme peril, to guarantee our security under the sun of liberty. Because of your bravery and alertness, we can enjoy the freedoms and tranquility we often take for granted. I applaud and thank those who have given their lives as the ultimate sacrifice. We will never be able to repay you for the highest acts of service that you have performed for us—your bravery and selflessness. The liberties and security we take daily for granted bear witness to your legacy.

Drs. Brian Pinzer, Jeffrey Davis, Stephen Grusendorf, Mary Lowe, Gary Bredfeldt, John Cartwright, Steve Lowe, Baylor Whitney, and Gabriel Etzel were among my distinguished Liberty University professors, from whom I had the honor of learning. You presented me with challenges that were essential to my growth and the attainment of my doctorate degree in education. I sincerely appreciate the time and work you put into helping me become the person I needed to be.

To the following pastors, their churches, and the incredible staff and volunteers—your ministry is a true testament to what it means to be a blessing to the community. Your friendship, leadership, and unwavering commitment to serving others are deeply appreciated. Your kindness and dedication set a powerful example, and I am grateful for the impact you make.

- Pastors Jeffrey and Nicola Smith – Strong Tower Church, Fredericksburg, Virginia
- Pastors Steve and Shawn Clark – MIEC, Majuro, Marshall Islands
- Pastors Jeff and Kim Connor – Haven Worship Center, Winter Haven, Florida
- Dr. Archie and Pastor Tangie Callahan – Bridge Church, Virginia Beach, Virginia
- Pastors Patrick "Packy" and Janet Thompson – Bayou Blue Assembly of God, Houma, Louisiana
- Bishop Michael and Pastor Kathi Pitts – Cornerstone Church, Toledo, Ohio

# INTRODUCTION

I began my official work in ministry in 1996 and preached my first sermon on September 21, 1997, at the Gospel Fellowship Outreach Worship Center (GFOWC) in Sicily, Italy. On October 12, 1998, I was ordained as a minister by GFOWC under Pastor Michael Smith. Following this, I was ordained as a minister under Higher Ground, Always Abounding Assemblies, on August 10, 1999, by Bishop T. D. Jakes and Bishop Watkins. My journey continued, and on April 7, 2002, I was ordained as a Pastor by Apostle Gregory Hunt at GFOWC. Most recently, I was ordained as an Apostle on February 19, 2022, under International Ministries, Christ His Power in Action, by Apostle Luciano Miranda and Pastor Mirasol Miranda.

More than twenty years ago, God gave me a clear understanding of why so many people leave churches when one or more of the "4 Ps" is absent. The "4 Ps"—Place, People, Praise, and Preaching—are essential cornerstones of establishing a church setting where people experience spiritual nourishment and community. When any of these components are lacking or inadequate, a person's experience is significantly impacted and can result in disengagement, reducing attendance.

Let's break down each of these "4 Ps" and how they affect church retention:

**Place**: The physical and spiritual environment of the church should be friendly, encouraging, and welcoming to promote a feeling of God's presence and community. People are more likely to be drawn to and stay in a welcoming setting.

**People**: Churches foster a sense of community, fostering friendship, support, and spiritual development. However, disengagement can occur when members feel isolated or alienated. The church should foster a sense of belonging and unity, preventing disengagement.

**Praise**: Praise and worship are vital in church life, uplifting the soul and fostering spiritual connection. Lifeless, uninspired praising can hinder worship, while sincere praise and worship create a stirring spiritual experience.

**Preaching**: The quality of sermons significantly influences a church's attendance or departure. Well-written sermons, grounded in scriptural principles, are compelling and relevant to the congregation's struggles, inspiring in-depth thought, and action. shallow sermons may cause disengagement and lower motivation to return.

When God revealed these to me, I was impressed by their profound simplicity and indisputable firmness. It became evident that individuals struggle to remain loyal to a church when there is a hole in their spiritual experience, a void typically caused by the weakening or lack of any of these foundational pillars: Place, People, Praise, and Preaching. Each component is essential for a spiritual journey to be fulfilling and transforming. A person experiences spiritual malnourishment and disconnection when these components are absent, rendering their total experience inadequate.

CHAPTER ONE

# PLACE

Often, we overlook the importance of the church's physical and spiritual surroundings. The setting should be friendly, cozy, and supportive of worship and community. This is about fostering an environment where people sense God's presence and a sense of belonging, not merely about convenience or aesthetics. People are less inclined to return if they perceive the space as chilly, unwelcoming, or chaotic. A church ought to offer a haven where individuals may flee from the chaos of everyday life and experience a sense of belonging to something bigger.

According to Ball (2020), two reasons in particular stand out in the article *15 Reasons Why Committed Christians Do Not Attend Church*: the belief that "church is boring" (#7) and the statement that "I don't know of any 'good' churches near me" (#10). These problems show how difficult it is for churches to connect with their members and build lasting community relationships. The notion that church might become boring reflects a larger social battle to keep worship sessions real and relevant. People are more likely to stop participating in religious activities when they do not align with their personal spirituality or lived experiences, according to research by Ammerman (2013) in *Congregations in America*. Like this, the difficulty in locating a "good" church reflects a perceived misalignment between one's personal values and church culture. Smith and Snell's (2009) *Souls in Transition* explores this issue and how religious participation is impacted by institutional trust and personal identity. To ensure that their services are spiritually enlightening, inclusive, and culturally relevant, congregations must innovate and adapt. This will help build stronger relationships with their communities.

The physical ambiance, lighting, seating configurations, and cleanliness can facilitate peace. This enables people to concentrate on worship without interruption. However, the spiritual atmosphere—which ought to convey an openness to God's presence—is more significant than aesthetics. People should feel like they are entering a sacred place when they enter a church that promotes introspection, prayer, and a closer relationship with God. Focusing on one's relationship with God and those around them is more straightforward when the environment is filled with love, warmth, and reverence.

A church should be more than just a building. It should be a haven, a place where people can temporarily forget about the problems of everyday life and find comfort in God's presence and in the fellowship of other believers. Creating a space where people feel comfortable being vulnerable, seeking healing, or celebrating happy moments is the goal here. In an unwelcoming or even hostile setting, people are less likely to find the spiritual nutrition they are looking for. They might feel disengaged, unsatisfied, or even alienated in such circumstances.

It is the duty of the entire congregation to foster a welcoming and spiritually uplifting environment, not only the leaders of the church. Creating a welcoming environment, exhibiting Christlike behavior, and fostering interpersonal relationships are all components of creating a place where others can feel like they belong. It's about creating an environment where God's love is evident, where unity flourishes, and where each person feels respected and welcomed—it's not simply about convenience or appearances. Our relationships with one another are what makes our church a community, not just a place of worship.

Essentially, a church's physical and spiritual environment ought to complement each other to produce a whole worship experience that deepens people's relationship with God and builds community. When these factors are in balance, people are significantly more likely to return and participate actively in the church's life and mission. However, the church may not offer people the solace and rejuvenation they frequently need without this balance. From the Tabernacle of Moses to the Tabernacle of David, from the splendor of the Temple of Solomon to the many synagogues that followed, today's churches have been brought together by the same goal: to house the Spirit of the Lord. Despite having different layouts, styles, and purposes, each of these structures aimed to provide a material and spiritual space where God's people may feel His presence. Over time, these areas represent the changing dynamic between God and His people, signifying their common yearning for spiritual contact.

Built-in the desert, the Tabernacle of Moses was a transportable tabernacle created by heavenly directives. Its function was to serve as a physical embodiment of God's covenant with His people and a place to hold religious ceremonies. The living God could be encountered there as He led the Israelites on their trek. The Tabernacle was a hallowed location where the Lord's Spirit might reside amid wandering people, reminding them of His ever-present presence despite their bodily movements. Every element of its architecture, including the altar and the Ark of the Covenant, was intended to promote this divine unity.

The Tabernacle of David followed, bringing an additional facet of worship. It was less formal and smaller in size than Moses' Tabernacle, yet it nonetheless represented a closer, more profound relationship with God. David, a man after God's heart, realized that worship invited the Lord to dwell among His people via constant praise, not just performing rituals. This was a location where worship was unrestricted by the rigid ceremonial customs of previous tabernacles, indicating a change toward a more approachable and intimate encounter with God the Spirit.

Next came the first permanent building erected in honor of the Lord, the magnificent and stupefying Temple of Solomon. Solomon's Temple, an architectural marvel, was the product of many years of religious devotion. Its elaborate design, adorned with gold, priceless stones, and expertly made items, conveyed the respect and honor rightfully due to the Almighty. The Temple, where sacrifices were offered, prayers were said, and the Holy of Holies housed the Spirit of God, was the focal point of Israel's religious life. God's glory poured upon the Temple so powerfully at its dedication that the priests could not stand and perform their duties (2 Chronicles 7:1-2). This incident revealed the building's actual function as a home, not just a location for ceremonies.

Synagogues became important centers of worship as history progressed, particularly when the Temple was destroyed, and the Jewish people were dispersed. These were neighborhood centers for fellowship, education, and religion. Their goal stayed the same, despite being less abundant than the Temple: to use group worship and scripture study to bring God's presence into the lives of His people. They were constructed so that the devout could still experience God's Spirit in their hearts without the actual Temple.

The fundamental goal of all these variations—from the Tabernacle in the desert to the synagogues in every community—has been constant: making room for the Spirit of the Lord to reside. These were holy locations intended for divine interaction, not just buildings. The goal was to provide a dwelling place for the living God, where He may live among His people and be experienced in their everyday lives, in addition to a place for worship.

Even now, this divine purpose remains relevant. Churches, temples, and other places of worship are still used as sanctuaries today, where people experience God's Spirit. But not just the building's exterior draws the Spirit within. What ultimately makes these locations holy is the community's devotion to reverence, praise, and prayer, as well as the worshipper's heart. God's desire to live among His people is found in the hearts of those who seek Him, not in walls or altars. The goal of the buildings is to provide a place where the Spirit of the Lord might dwell, leading people closer to Him in every generation, even though the buildings themselves may change.

## THE TABERNACLE OF MOSES

Throughout the Israelites' forty-year desert trek, the LORD lived in the tabernacle—a finely built, transportable tent that provided a holy area for prayer, sacrifice, and intimate communion with God. This sacred building served as their Temple until they could enter the promised land. The Tabernacle is unique because God designed it and gave Moses detailed directions for building it, including requirements for size, materials, and furnishings. The requirements (*New International Version*, 2024, Exodus 25:1–40) underscore the importance of beauty, symbolism, and reverence in worship, highlighting God's desire for a physical home among His people.

Every element of the Tabernacle held profound spiritual importance, from the Ark of the Covenant, which symbolized God's presence and covenant with His people, to the various altars and the inner sanctum known as the Holy of Holies. The tabernacle was designed for easy assembly and disassembly, reflecting God's willingness to accompany His people during their travels and His desire for an intimate relationship. The descriptions' purposeful repetition of details highlights the significance of each element, highlighting the value of reverence and attention in worship.

The Tabernacle of Moses was a significant structure in the religious life of the Israelites. It served as a mobile dwelling place for God during their journey through the wilderness. Detailed in the Book of Exodus, the Tabernacle consisted of numerous major components, each with its own spiritual importance and practical use.

## *The Outer Court*

When one first entered the Tabernacle complex, they were greeted by the outer court. It was encircled with a tall linen fence and was roughly 150 feet by 75 feet (45 meters by 22.5 meters) (Exodus 27:9-19). The Israelites could approach God while feeling reverent because the outer court acted as a transitional area between the sacred and the common.

The Bronze Altar, the site of sacrifices, existed here. This altar was 7.5 feet square and 4.5 feet high, constructed of acacia wood covered in brass (Exodus 27:1-2). It represented the forgiveness of sins and the need for sacrifice to have a relationship with God (Merrill, 2000).

## *The Holy Place (Inner Court)*

The Holy Place, a two-part tent structure, was outside the outer court. The dimensions of the Holy Place were thirty feet by fifteen feet and fifteen feet high (Exodus 26:15-30). It was equipped with three main things:

- **The Golden Lampstand (Menorah)**: According to Exodus 25:31–40, this seven-branched, pure gold lampstand illuminated the Holy Place. According to Freedman (2000), the lampstand represented God's presence and the light of His Word, directing the Israelites on their spiritual journey.
- **The Table of Showbread**: This table, covered in gold and made of acacia wood, held twelve loaves of bread, which stood for the twelve tribes of Israel (Exodus 25:23-30). The

bread was replaced every week, signifying God's supply, and the food He provides for His people (Ferguson, 1999).

- **The Altar of Incense**: This little altar, which stood directly in front of the Holy of Holies door, was used by worshippers to burn incense (Exodus 30:1–10). According to Wenham (2008), the sweet smoke symbolized the people's prayers ascending to God, highlighting the significance of prayer in the relationship between God and His people.

## *The Holy of Holies*

The Holy of Holies, a hallowed area that measured 15 feet by 15 feet, was the most interior section of the Tabernacle (Exodus 26:31–33). The most important object in the Tabernacle, the Ark of the Covenant, was kept in this section. The tablets of the Ten Commandments, Aaron's rod, and a container of manna were all kept in the Ark, a wooden chest covered in gold (Exodus 25:10–22; Hebrews 9:4).

Per Exodus 25:17–22, the Ark held the Mercy Seat, a solid gold cover with two cherubim on either side. It stood in for both God's throne and His presence's location among the Israelites. Once a year on the Day of Atonement, the High Priest would enter the Holy of Holies and sprinkle the blood of a sacrificed lamb on the Mercy Seat, symbolizing atonement for the sins of the people (Leviticus 16:2-34) (Merrill, 2000).

Ultimately, the tabernacle represented more than just a tangible tower; it was essential to the covenantal bond between God and Israel. As the Israelites faced the difficulties of the wilderness, it provided a sense of purity and camaraderie while acting as a site for sacrifice, worship, and atonement. It also served as a reminder of God's promises. Its emphasis during this time reflects its crucial role in forming the Israelites' spiritual identity and creating a foundation for their connection with God.

## THE TABERNACLE OF DAVID

The religious ceremonies of ancient Israel underwent a substantial change with the construction of the Tabernacle of David. The Tabernacle of David functioned as a more permanent place of worship than the earlier Tabernacle of Moses, a transportable tent intended for the Israelites' trek through the desert. It was built to hold the Ark of the Covenant in Jerusalem, and it's frequently linked to a new style of worship that prioritized praise, music, and social interaction.

### *The Ark of the Covenant*

The Ark of the Covenant, a representation of God's presence among His people, was in the center of the Tabernacle of David. The Ten Commandments were inscribed on stone tablets, there was a pot of manna, and Aaron's rod was inside the acacia wood and gold-overlaid Ark (Exodus 25:10–22). King David carried the Ark to Jerusalem, where it became the center of attention in his tabernacle, as recorded in 2 Samuel 6:2. Because the Ark was kept in a tent, it symbolized a tight bond between God and His people. It acted as a continual reminder of His covenantal obligations.

## *The Tent Structure*

In contrast to the elaborate design of the previous Tabernacle of Moses, the actual tent structure of the Tabernacle of David was relatively straightforward. Presumably, it was a more accessible and open area that promoted group worship and meetings. Although the precise architectural characteristics are not well documented, the tent promoted people's participation in worship and allowed for a more intimate interaction with God. This tent represented God's desire to live among and be approachable by His people (1 Chronicles 15:1).

## *Worship and Music*

The Tabernacle of David was distinguished by its emphasis on praise and singing as a means of worship. The singers and musicians were a group of Levites that David sent to lead the assembly in worship (1 Chronicles 6:31-32). This comprised playing various musical instruments, including cymbals, harps, and lyres, which added to the lively and exuberant atmosphere of praise. A more intimate and communal way of connecting with God was emphasized by the pioneering introduction of structured musical worship (Willem A. Vaneferin, 1997).

## *Sacrifices and Offerings*

The Tabernacle of David preserved the custom of making sacrifices as a form of devotion and atonement in addition to singing. An essential part of Israelite worship, these offerings represented the need for atonement and peace with God (1 Chronicles 16:1). David made great sacrifices *to* dedicate the Tabernacle, demonstrating his devotion and the value of worship in the community's spiritual life.

## *Spiritual Significance*

Israelite worship underwent a change with the construction of the Tabernacle of David, moving from a centralized ceremonial style to a more inclusive and expressive one. It underlined the value of community involvement and the delight of worshiping God. This change predicted later developments in Jewish worship, especially when Solomon, David's son, built the Temple, formalizing and extending the customs started in David's Tabernacle (Willem A. Vaneferin, 1997).

An important turning point in Israelite worship history was the Tabernacle of David, which symbolized a shift toward a closer, more intimate relationship with God. The foundation for later worship customs in ancient Israel and abroad was established by housing the Ark of the Covenant and placing a strong emphasis on music and group worship.

## THE TEMPLE OF SOLOMON

One of the most important inventions in the history of ancient Israelite religion is the First Temple, also known as the Temple of Solomon. Built in the eleventh century BCE, it served as both the permanent home for the Ark of the Covenant and the center of Israelite devotion.

## Historical Context

David wanted to build a temple for God, and King Solomon fulfilled his wish and built the Temple of Solomon. But God told David that his son would finish this work (2 Samuel 7:12–13). Solomon's reign is renowned for its peace and prosperity, providing the perfect environment for such a massive undertaking. 1 Kings 6-7 and 2 Chronicles 3–4 describe the Temple's construction, emphasizing its grandeur and importance in Israel's history.

## Architectural Design

The Phoenician and Egyptian architectural styles impacted the Temple of Solomon, indicating the cross-cultural interactions of that era. The Temple, which stood on Mount Moriah in Jerusalem, was roughly sixty cubits in length, twenty cubits in width, and thirty cubits in height (1 Kings 6:2). The framework was made up of various essential parts:

- **The Holy of Holies:** A veil divided the innermost chamber, which held the Ark of the Covenant, from the remainder of the Temple (1 Kings 6:19–20). It was considered the most hallowed place on earth, where God resided.
- **The Holy Place:** according to 1 Kings 7:48, this bigger space housed the Altar of Incense, the Golden Lampstand

(Menorah), and the Table of Showbread. The priests used it as a place to carry out sacrifices and rites.

- **The Sea of Bronze Basin,** where the priests washed before entering the Temple, and the Bronze Altar for burnt offerings were in the courtyard (2 Chronicles 4:1). The people might congregate for worship outside.

## Materials and Construction

Superior building materials and expert labor were used to construct the Temple of Solomon. Solomon hired the expert artisan Hiram of Tyre to help build the Temple (1 Kings 7:13–14). The Temple was constructed of limestone, gold ornamentation, and Lebanon cedar wood. The descriptions of the Temple's furniture and decorations, including elaborate carvings and gold overlays, demonstrate the meticulous craftsmanship and attention to detail (1 Kings 6:15-22).

## Religious Significance

The Israelites' primary location of worship, the Temple of Solomon, strengthened their covenantal bond with God. As required by the Mosaic Law, it served as the principal site for festivals, sacrifices, and meetings (Deuteronomy 12:5-7). The Temple, representing God's presence and desire to live among His people, was extremely important to the nation's spiritual life. When Solomon dedicated it, he prayed fervently, imploring God to hear the people's prayers and pardon their sins when they turned toward the Temple (2

Chronicles 6:24-31). The Temple's importance as a location where the locals might commune with God and ask for His direction was highlighted by this dedication.

## *The Temple's Legacy*

A pivotal point in Jewish history, the Temple of Solomon stood for almost 400 years till the Babylonians destroyed it in 586 BCE. For the Israelites, its destruction signified not just the loss of the building's physical construction but also a serious spiritual crisis. The Second Temple, constructed following the Babylonian exile, carried on the Temple's tradition, and continues to be a crucial component of Jewish identity and worship today (Josephus, 1981). An outstanding accomplishment in ancient Israel, the Temple of Solomon, resulted from architectural mastery, cultural impact, and religious devotion. The building of it and its significance highlights the role that worship played in Israelite community life and its lasting influence on Jewish history.

## SYNAGOGUES

An important turning point in the history of Israelite religious practice was the establishment of synagogues as hubs for Jewish worship, education, and communal life. Following the demolition of Solomon's Temple and the ensuing exile in Babylon, synagogues emerged as crucial locations for group worship and education.

## *The Historical Context:*

The Babylonian Empire's destruction of Solomon's Temple in 586 BCE, which significantly impacted Jewish religious life, is intimately linked to establishing synagogues (2 Kings 25:8-9). Since King Solomon had built the Temple, it had been the Israelites' primary site of devotion and sacrifice (1 Kings 6:1). A significant portion of the Jewish population was forced to flee Jerusalem and the surrounding areas because of its destruction and the accompanying Babylonian captivity, leaving the people without a central place of prayer. The center of the Jewish people's religious and communal life, the Temple, was destroyed when they were exiled to Babylon. When the Jewish people lost access to their customary forms of worship, like sacrifices and temple rites, they started to meet in small groups to pray, study the Torah, and uphold their religious identity. Worship based around the Temple began to give way to communal meetings around Scripture and prayer during this time (Psalm 137:1-4). These assemblies prepared the way for the founding of synagogues.

## *The Emergence of Synagogues in Exile*

Throughout ancient Babylon and other Near Eastern areas, where the Israelites were scattered, synagogues became centers of communal gatherings for learning, prayer, and organizing. The synagogue is referred to in Hebrew as *Beit Knesset*, which means "house of assembly," emphasizing its significance as a venue for social gatherings. Unlike the Temple, which was primarily a place for sacrificial worship, synagogues emphasized the reading and interpretation of the Torah, prayer, and instruction in the Law (Nehemiah 8:1-8). One of the first records of these public assemblies may be found in the book of Ezekiel, one of the exiles in Babylon. To hear visions and communications from the Lord, Ezekiel and the elders of Judah sat in a home (Ezekiel 8:1). This assembly, while not officially designated as a synagogue, served as a model for the subsequently established organization. The lack of a temple required the development of a new kind of worship that would make study and group reading of the Bible the main activities of synagogue life.

## *The Role of Synagogues After the Return from Exile*

The Second Temple was built in 516 BCE, after the Persian ruler Cyrus permitted the Jews to return to Jerusalem and construct the Temple (Ezra 1:1–4). Yet, synagogues remained an important part of Jewish communities. For those who chose not to return to Jerusalem, synagogues remained the central hub for prayer and education. Synagogues spread across Jerusalem, acting as additional places of worship and study, especially on the Sabbath and other communal events (Acts 13:14–15). Further background is given by the book of Nehemiah, which tells the story of Ezra, the scribe, reciting the Law in front of the people following the Temple's reconstruction (Nehemiah 8:1–12). This event, which happened outside the Temple, emphasizes how important it is becoming to teach and read the Torah aloud in public settings. A distinguishing feature of synagogue worship was its concentration on comprehending and elucidating the Scriptures, in contrast to the Temple's emphasis on sacrifices and ceremonial purity.

## The Expansion of Synagogues

During the Intertestamental Period synagogues were firmly established as essential institutions in Jewish society throughout the Intertestamental Period (the time between the Old and New Testaments) in Israel and the Jewish Diaspora. During this time, a group of Jewish educators and leaders known as Pharisees emerged, emphasizing the value of studying the Law and the significance of synagogues as hubs for learning and spiritual development. Synagogues had grown widely by the time of Jesus and the apostle Paul, acting as hubs for social events, communal prayer, and education. Jesus' teachings in synagogues in Galilee and Judea are mentioned multiple times in the Gospels (Matthew 4:23; Luke 4:16). Paul's missionary approach of beginning his work in neighborhood synagogues, where he would preach and interact with both Jews and Gentile God-fearers, is also highlighted in the book of Acts (Acts 17:1-2).

## Synagogue Structure and Function

A synagogue's basic layout included a main hall for prayer and Torah reading, with seats set around the bema, or center platform, where the texts were read and discussed. The Torah scrolls were normally kept in a chest called the ark, a common feature in synagogues. Beyond just being a place of worship, the synagogue also functioned as a place of learning, prayer, and assembly, among other civic and religious duties (Mark 1:21).

## Religious and Cultural Significance

The construction of synagogues signaled a significant change in Jewish religious worship and identity. Jews could now pray in their local communities without being dependent on a single central temple, which increased accessibility and participation. Particularly in the face of exile and dispersion, this decentralization of worship preserved Jewish faith and identity. In addition to being a place of learning and prayer, the synagogue grew to represent flexibility and resiliency in the Jewish faith (Lee, 2014).

Jewish worship traditions underwent a significant shift with the construction of synagogues following the collapse of Solomon's Temple. These tiny gatherings during the Babylonian exile grew into well-established centers of religious life by the time of the Second Temple and beyond. Their ascent demonstrated the importance of communal life, education, and prayer while ensuring the survival of Jewish religious and cultural identity in the absence of a central temple.

## Contemporary Churches

Beginning with the synagogue system established during the Babylonian exile, the development of the early Christian community, and finally the evolution of modern Christian worship spaces, the evolution of modern churches can be traced back through several historical and theological shifts. Each stage marks an important transition in how religious communities gathered, worshiped, and structured their communal life.

## *Synagogues as Precursors to Christian Worship Spaces*

As mentioned, synagogues developed during the exile in Babylon and became essential to Jewish community life, prayer, and worship (Nehemiah 8:1–12). Synagogues were common by the time of Jesus, serving as hubs for prayer and education in Israel and throughout the Jewish Diaspora (Matthew 4:23; Acts 13:14-15). The emergence of Christian worship facilities was primarily shaped by the model of synagogues, which arranged communal meetings around teaching, prayer, and scripture reading. Initially, worshiping and learning about Jesus occurred in synagogues, where many early Jewish Christians congregated. However, when Christianity spread and set itself apart from Judaism, the early adherents gathered for worship in private houses. These meetings, which are often called "house churches," were essential to the formation of Christian worship in the early years (Romans 16:3-5; Acts 2:46). The growing hostility between Jewish authorities and the early Christian community, which ultimately resulted in a formal split between the two groups, contributed to this transition from synagogue to house church.

## House Churches and Early Christian Worship

According to the New Testament, Christians mostly gathered in private houses throughout the first several centuries following the life of Jesus (Acts 2:46; Romans 16:5). Believers would congregate in these tiny, personal house churches for friendship, prayer, communion (breaking of bread), and apostles' teachings. House churches were structured similarly to synagogues, emphasizing Scripture, instruction, and group prayer, but with a special focus on the teachings of Jesus Christ and the Lord's Supper. The early Jerusalem Christian community "broke bread in their homes and ate together with glad and sincere hearts," according to the book of Acts (Acts 2:46, NIV). Early Christian assemblies were characterized by this aspect of collective worship. However, as the Christian community expanded and dispersed over the Roman Empire, the need for larger, more formal halls of worship became apparent. Some wealthy Christians started building specialized Christian worship structures or offering larger spaces around the third century.

## Christianity's Legalization and the Growth of Church Structures

When Emperor Constantine issued the **Edict of Milan** in 313 A.D., legalizing Christianity across the Roman Empire, it marked a dramatic shift in the evolution of Christian places of worship. Christians have before frequently been persecuted and compelled to gather in secret. The legalization of Christianity allowed for the public construction of churches and gave Christian communities safety. Rome's public structures of the same name served as the model for the first significant Christian churches, or basilicas. These vast, open spaces were great for gathering large congregations. One of the most well-known examples of these early Christian church structures is the Basilica of Saint Peter in Rome, built during Constantine's reign in the fourth century. A central nave with side aisles, an apse housing the altar, and a narthex, or gathering place for worshippers, were common features of basilicas. For generations, church architecture has been influenced by this fundamental architectural shape (Ferguson, 2013). Christian worship changed from being intimate, private meetings to grand, open rituals with the advent of house churches and vast public basilicas. More complex liturgical practices, including processions, choirs, and the use of holy art and symbols to enhance prayer, were made possible by this shift.

## *The Development of Church Architecture During the Middle Ages*

Building churches and cathedrals became an important way for Christians to show their faith and dedication during the Middle Ages, especially in Europe. With their imposing spires, elaborate stone carvings, and stained-glass windows, Gothic cathedrals were constructed as architectural symbols of God's splendor and Christian doctrine. These buildings were often constructed over the course of several generations, serving as places of worship, pilgrimage, and community life. Christian worship evolved into a more hierarchical structure throughout this time, with the clergy assuming more official positions in service leadership. This developing division was reflected in the division of the nave (for congregants) and the chancel (for clergy). Churches continued to play an important role in communal life, serving as hubs for social services, education, and even government in addition to being houses of worship (Kilde, 2008).

## The Protestant Reformation and the Simplification of Church Spaces

The 16th-century Protestant Reformation significantly altered church architecture and worship customs. Reformers like Martin Luther and John Calvin placed more emphasis on preaching and Scripture than the ornate rituals of the Catholic Church. Protestant church architecture consequently became more straightforward, emphasizing the pulpit and Scripture reading above the altar and sacraments. Churches that mirrored the theological emphasis on direct access to God via faith and the Word were also built because of the Reformation. Rather than the standing crowds of older church designs, pews were a standard element of Protestant churches, allowing attendees to sit and listen to lengthy sermons.

## Current Churches

Church architecture has changed throughout the modern era to reflect societal changes and modify worship styles. To meet the demands of expanding congregations, some modern churches, especially those in the Protestant and evangelical traditions, have adopted minimalist designs with spacious, open layouts, basic furnishings, and cutting-edge technology like sound systems and video screens. On the other hand, certain denominations—especially those in Catholicism and Orthodoxy—have stuck to more conventional styles, emphasizing liturgical space, icons, and holy art. Churches now function as hubs for social justice, education, and community involvement in addition to being places of worship. The synagogue and house church were locations where believers gathered to worship God, study Scripture, and serve their communities. The modern church continues this history by fusing old customs and cutting-edge technologies.

The way that churches have evolved from the synagogue system shows how flexible Christian worship may be over time. Churches have been molded by theological, cultural, and historical reasons while preserving their primary purpose as venues for communal worship and spiritual formation. These spaces include house churches, vast basilicas, Gothic cathedrals, and contemporary worship centers.

# CHAPTER ONE SUMMARY

This chapter examines the development of sacred spaces within the framework of religious worship. It starts with the idea of a building fund. It proceeds to historical locations such as the **Temple of Solomon**, the **Tabernacle of David**, and the **Tabernacle of Moses** before moving on to **synagogues and** contemporary or **modern-day churches**. Every segment showcases key junctures in the evolution of collective worship and emphasizes the theological and cultural transformations that influenced these environments.

## THE BUILDING FUND

**The Building Fund** is a continuous endeavor by the modern church to provide funding for the construction or repair of places of worship. It highlights the difficulties many congregations have in finding the money to build new places of worship or renovate and maintain their current ones. These donations are frequently made over an extended period, and the lack of clarity or transparency regarding the overall amount raised or the intended purpose can cause confusion and irritation. In constructing projects that function as hubs for community and worship, this section emphasizes the significance of vision and accountability.

## THE TABERNACLE OF MOSES

**The Tabernacle of Moses** was constructed by the divine directions provided to Moses, and it served as God's first temporary home (Exodus 25:1–40:38). It was intended to be a transportable sanctuary that the Israelites would take on their forty-year desert expedition. Specific components, including the Holy of Holies, the Ark of the Covenant, the altar of burnt offerings, and the table of showbread, made up the tabernacle. These objects had great symbolic meaning; they stood for God's presence, covenant, and the system of sacrifice that allowed Israel to atone for sin. God's wish to live among His people was mirrored in the Tabernacle's intricate design, setting a precedent for holy places prioritizing intentionality and reverence in worship.

## THE TABERNACLE OF DAVID

**The Tabernacle of David** symbolizes a change in Israel's religious customs. King David built a new, more permanent building in Jerusalem to hold the Ark of the Covenant after the Tabernacle of Moses had served its function (2 Samuel 6:17). Despite being more straightforward than Moses' Tabernacle, David's nonetheless functioned as the center of worship, emphasizing instruments, music, and praise above all else. David brought in a more joyous worship style featuring constant prayer, singing, and God's real presence. This tabernacle represented the changing relationship between God and His people and stressed the need for worship as a dynamic, ongoing experience.

# The Temple of Solomon

**The Temple of Solomon**, constructed by King Solomon, represented the culmination of Israel's desire for a permanent, grand house of worship. When the Temple in Jerusalem was built, it replaced the Tabernacle of David as the main venue for Jewish prayer and sacrifice (1 Kings 6). The Temple was a magnificent building that was built in accordance with divine requirements. It had altars, courts, and elaborate decorations in addition to the Holy of Holies, which held the Ark of the Covenant. The Temple served as Israel's governmental and spiritual hub and represented God's constant presence among His people. Jews' conception of worship and exile was shaped by its destruction and subsequent reconstruction, which occurred during crucial periods in Jewish history.

# Synagogues

**Synagogues -** the Jewish people established synagogues as centers of worship, learning, and social interaction after the Babylonians destroyed the First Temple and drove them into exile (Nehemiah 8:1–12). The local, dispersed worship of synagogues, as opposed to the centralized worship of the Temple, allowed Jewish communities to continue practicing their religion even after they were divided from Jerusalem. Particularly during the Babylonian exile and in the Jewish Diaspora, synagogues became crucial for teaching the Torah, worshiping, and promoting social life. The synagogue model has significantly impacted Christian worship traditions, especially regarding the focus placed on Scripture reading, teaching, and group prayer (Luke 4:16; Acts 13:14).

## CURRENT CHURCHES

**Current churches** from these ancient forms, modern churches developed, absorbing aspects from the synagogue, the earliest Christian home churches, and more ornate constructions like the basilicas constructed following the Roman Empire's legalization of Christianity. For worship, fellowship, and the Eucharist, the early Christians first gathered in houses (Acts 2:46; Romans 16:5). The design and purpose of churches have changed over the ages, with significant changes occurring during the Reformation and the globalization of Christianity. Today, Churches represent centuries of theological, cultural, and architectural growth, serving as places of worship and hubs for volunteerism.

CHAPTER TWO

# PEOPLE

In addition to the preaching and worship style, a church's ability to cultivate a strong feeling of community frequently draws people in. The ties and relationships forged inside a congregation are fundamental to why people decide to stay faithful to a specific church. Members are more inclined to attend regularly and participate in church activities when they feel genuinely recognized, loved, and supported. Church becomes a spiritual home where friendships are nourished, life's struggles are shared, and personal development is fostered. It becomes more than just a location to attend services.

The congregation's warmth, support, and friendliness are essential to fostering a sense of belonging. The church's members are critical to providing hospitality and creating a sense of belonging for frequent visitors and newcomers. A loving and accepting church community fosters an atmosphere where people feel free to express who they are, discuss their struggles, and look to the church for spiritual direction. This transparency encourages relationships to develop that go beyond fleeting exchanges and offer ongoing emotional and spiritual support.

On the other hand, it could be challenging for someone to maintain a connection when they feel alone or unwanted. Even longtime members may feel scrutinized or alienated if the church is cruel, uncaring, or exclusive. In these situations, people could feel like outsiders rather than appreciated church family members. They can think that their problems and contributions are not valued, or their presence is not valued. Disengagement may result from this lack of connection since people gravitate toward groups where they are accepted and feel like they belong.

Every churchgoer has a responsibility to help create a community where everyone is valued and feels connected to a more excellent spiritual family. This is building relationships via sincere communication, whether in small groups, at social gatherings, or just by smiling and saying hello on a Sunday morning. Churches flourish when their members live life together, experiencing each other's pleasures and difficulties in addition to worshiping together. People are likelier to stick around in such an environment because they feel like an essential part of something bigger than themselves.

However, a church's lack of ties or sentiments of division can cause disenchantment and disengagement. The atmosphere of love and unity is undermined if cliques take over or conflict festers, and people could decide to leave the church in quest of a more welcoming and peaceful neighborhood. Without connection, the church can no longer look like the loving spiritual family it is intended to be but rather like another impersonal organization. For this reason, fostering enduring, caring relationships within the congregation is essential to the development and well-being of any church community. The thirteenth reason, "I've been hurt by church members," emphasizes the significance of interpersonal conflict within religious communities, according to Ball's article, *15 Reasons Why Committed Christians Do Not Attend Church*. In conversations concerning church attendance, this phrase highlights a common theme: the depressing consequences of unsolved conflicts, perceived hypocrisy, or abuse inside congregational settings. To save their emotional health, people may withdraw from the church because of painful experiences.

The idea that unresolved conflict within a congregation frequently leads to falling attendance and disengagement is supported by scholarly research. Interpersonal interactions within religious societies are essential in promoting loyalty or estrangement, claim Smith and Snell (2009). People's willingness to stay participating can be significantly impacted by negative experiences, such as feeling mistreated or judged. This argument emphasizes how crucial it is to help church communities develop a culture of forgiveness, compassion, and amicable dispute resolution. To promote reconciliation and avoid additional disillusionment, leaders and members alike must work to establish an atmosphere in which complaints may be handled politely.

People are essential not just in daily life but also in the church community. Whether newcomers feel welcome and decide to stay is largely determined by the environment that the congregation and staff create. The right attitude of friendliness and love is crucial, as people are less inclined to return to a church if it's lacking. Often, newcomers seek something more than just a place to worship; they want a place to connect, grow, and feel supported like family members. A more cohesive and muscular body of believers is fostered in a church where members can form relationships, share knowledge, and rely on one another. Even the most excellent sermons or programs might not be able to give individuals looking for spiritual connection a lasting, meaningful experience if there is not this inclusive and compassionate attitude.

## POWER IN NUMBERS

Expanding on the notion that people might utilize a church building as a gateway to enter a community, it's critical to realize that a church's physical layout is more than just its walls and floors; it serves as a haven where people can escape the stresses of the outside world. For many people, becoming a church provides a concrete means of establishing a connection with a religious community that maintains principles of accountability, love, and support. According to Miller (2008), the obligation to uphold morally upright and spiritually inspired standards in a religious setting can strongly resist outside temptations (pg. 165). According to this theory, those looking for moral stability and spiritual development might feel comfortable having the church community as their protector. It substitutes for the ambiguity and difficulties frequently encountered in the larger, materialistic society.

This sense of safety and belonging is enhanced by being around sincere believers who are Christians. A religious community provides a sense of shared purpose, in contrast to secular societies' competitive and frequently isolating aspects. People who are believers can rely on the combined power of other believers, strengthening their bond with God and one another. People feel "safer" in this atmosphere—both physically and spiritually— because they are a part of a community that supports them in leading lives consistent with their beliefs.

Furthermore, " through Christ" can Christians access this unique bond with one another. Lowe & Lowe (2018) emphasize that through Christ, believers experience a more profound connection that allows for access, joy, and fellowship with one another (pg. 176). The Christian community is known for its spiritual oneness, which allows members to rejoice in collective worship, rejoice in one another's successes, and encourage one another through difficult times. The barriers of separation and loneliness are dismantled by Christ, allowing genuine connections to thrive. In a community like this, individuals feel seen, heard, and loved—a reflection of Christ's unfailing love for everyone.

Essentially, the church serves as a protective shield, shielding Christians from the challenges and distractions of the outside world. It provides a secure setting for spiritual development, offering members both accountability and camaraderie. The encouragement and support of fellow believers can act as a moral compass, guiding individuals away from the temptations of daily life.

As a result, the church building serves as more than just a venue for religious events; it also serves as a doorway to a more satisfying life in Christ. It provides a space where people can find acceptance, spiritual support, and the group willpower to overcome life's challenges since they realize they are not alone but rather members of a wider religious community.

# THE WHOLE ARMOR OF GOD

Sermons on the complete armor of God, especially those based on the epistle to the Ephesians, have long been a mainstay of Christian doctrine. This verse, which is frequently read individually, highlights that it is each believer's unique duty to "put on the whole armor of God" in order to withstand spiritual attacks (Ephesians 6:11, NIV). Traditionally, the emphasis has been on how each Christian must arm oneself independently to face trials and spiritual warfare with spiritual armor, which includes truth, righteousness, peace, faith, salvation, and God's Word. Thoughts have recently turned to comprehending this potent metaphor in a business setting. From the perspective of corporate faith, the consequences are significant: when all members of a church, not just a select few, are fully clothed in God's armor, the church ceases to be a group of isolated believers engaged in solo combat and becomes a unified army moving forward in spiritual warfare.

Paul, the apostle, emphasizes in Ephesians 6:10–18 that Christians must "be strong in the Lord and in His mighty power" and that they should arm themselves with all of God's armor. This is a metaphor that has great significance for both individual and group spiritual battle. Although the traditional interpretation of this armor has been interpreted as a call for individual spiritual preparedness, a closer look reveals that Paul's teachings have significant consequences for the church, the corporate body of Christ. This verse, when interpreted in the context of a community, demands a united, group spiritual offensive and defense that goes beyond individual conflict.

## *The Armor of God: Corporate Impact*

### The Belt of Truth

Since it keeps the other pieces of armor together, the belt of truth is fundamental. Within a personal setting, this work signifies a dedication to honesty and moral rectitude. In a corporate setting, on the other hand, honesty, openness, and trust are what bind the whole church together under the belt of truth. A church girded with truth creates an environment that is hostile to falsehood and hypocrisy. Relationships and ministries are constructed on a shared foundation of truth, which guarantees that all actions are based in God's truth and not on cultural or personal distortions. Paul emphasizes in Ephesians 6:14, NIV, "Stand firm then, with the belt of truth buckled around your waist." This reality binds the body together and establishes an accountable community where people support one another in honesty.

### The Breastplate of Righteousness

The breastplate of righteousness, which stands for moral rectitude and integrity, shields the heart. As it protects the individual from sin and transgression, the breastplate in the corporate body covers the church's collective heart. It keeps the entire body of the church safe from corruption and moral compromise by ensuring that its goals and deeds are in line with God's standards of righteousness. A community that is clothed in righteousness protects its witness to the world by reflecting the sanctity and purity of God as a whole. Paul notes that this righteousness is not only human effort but rather the righteousness that Christ has imputed, giving the church the strength to withstand attacks on its moral integrity.

## The Shield of Faith

One of the most important pieces of armor is perhaps the shield of faith, which is meant to stop the "flaming arrows of the evil one" (Ephesians 6:16, NIV). In a personal sense, it symbolizes the believer's faith in God's promises. But Paul's picture also points to a corporate application for the shield. To create a nearly impenetrable barrier, troops would link their shields to form a protective phalanx during ancient battle. Like this, the church creates a collective defense against doubt, fear, and spiritual attacks when it raises the shield of faith collectively. Collectively, their faith fortifies and uplifts one another, making them more resilient to the enemy's attacks than any one believer could be.

## Feet with Gospel of Peace

Ephesians 6:15 describes the Gospel of Peace, which is a vital component of the spiritual armor that Paul exhorts believers to put on. Having our feet "fitted with the readiness that comes from the gospel of peace" is how it is specifically described (NIV). This component is a symbolic exhortation to believers to be rooted and ready to resist in the spiritual struggles they encounter while sharing the good news of peace that the gospel offers. This gospel of peace's "preparation" implies that believers should be ready and prepared to hold fast and share this message wherever they go.

The picture of feet wearing this gospel suggests that one should be mobile and prepared to go and spread the word.

## The Helmet of Salvation

The confidence of salvation and hope in Christ are symbolized by the helmet of salvation, which guards the mind. Wearing this helmet represents the church's belief that each member is firmly rooted in their understanding of salvation and that they all share the same aspiration of eternal life. With this certainty, the church is protected from doctrinal errors, doubt attacks that can weaken and divide the body, and fear of damnation. The "hope of salvation" is symbolized by the helmet, as Paul states in another epistle (1 Thessalonians 5:8, NIV), and when a church is secure in this hope, it advances fearlessly and is not deterred by doubt or fear.

## The Sword of the Spirit

The only offensive weapon in the armor is the sword of the Spirit, which is the Bible (Ephesians 6:17, NIV). Sword by sword, believers can use the truth of Scripture to sever lies and deception. But the Word of God gains even greater potency when it is applied by the entire church, acting as a collective spiritual weapon. A Bible-based church can instruct, chastise, correct, and provide training in righteousness (2 Timothy 3:16, NIV). God's Word, when preached and applied collectively, becomes a transformational force that advances God's kingdom and drives back the powers of evil.

## The Power of Corporate Armor

When the church is seen as a whole, the armor of God turns it from a collection of disparate people engaged in personal conflict into a cohesive force that engages in spiritual combat. Paul's larger point in Ephesians 4:3-6 about the oneness of the body of Christ is reflected in this group's strength. The church is better equipped with the armor to protect itself from outside assaults and to grow in integrity, purpose, and spiritual development. When the whole church puts on God's armor, it advances and becomes a powerful force.

Ephesians 6:10–18, which describes the whole armor of God, calls the church to come together as one body, fully equipped for the spiritual conflicts it faces. It goes beyond personal readiness. By using the Word of God as a common weapon, the church may establish an environment of truth, righteousness, faith, and hope as it collectively dons this armor. Because of its oneness, the church is better able to hold firm and advance as a unit under God's might. The church uses the armor to not only defend itself but also to progress, sharing the gospel and enlarging God's reign on earth.

The church moves from individual spiritual combat to group spiritual growth when it operates as a single army, with every member donning all of God's armor. The church becomes a powerful force that unites in hardship, with one believer supporting the other, rather than fighting wars alone. Paul emphasizes the oneness of the body of Christ in Ephesians, and this mirrors his larger message there as well: "Make every effort to keep the unity of the Spirit through the bond of peace." "One Spirit and One Body" (Ephesians 4:3–4, NIV). As the body of Christ, the church needs to work together to pursue righteousness and spiritual development, encouraging one another while fighting spiritual battles.

If we look at the armor of God from a corporate standpoint, we see that the church is a cohesive, spiritually equipped army rather than merely a group of individual warriors. When the armor is worn in unison, its efficacy is increased, strengthening defenses, and accelerating God's work. The corporate aspect of God's armor serves as more evidence that believers must stand firmly together as a united front in spiritual warfare rather than fighting it alone.

## GOD IS LOVE

Many of the songs I heard growing up in church helped me grow my faith; some were taken straight from the Bible. One particularly noteworthy song is based on 1 John 4:7-8: "Beloved, let us show love to one another; for love is of God, and God is known by those who are loving. As God is love, he who does not love does not know God (*King James Version*, 2024, 1 John 4:7-8). This chapter, frequently sung during church services, conveys an important lesson about what Christian love is all about. It serves as a reminder that love reflects God's nature rather than just a feeling. Since God is the very incarnation of love, to know God is to know love. The core of a person's faith is demonstrated by their love for others, demonstrating their communion with God. However, the lack of love in a person's deeds and heart begs the question of how well they understand God since the Bible states, "He that loveth not Knoweth not God."

When this passage is set to music, it becomes a melody for the soul as well as the ears, pushing believers to reflect on their own behavior and hearts. It reminds us that love is the foundation of our relationships with God and one another. The words' seeming simplicity belies their profound meaning, calling us to live a life based on love and reveal God's presence in how we treat others. As we sing these lines, we are reminded that love for one another is not only required of us but also a reflection of God, calling us to embody the idea that "God is love."

When people first walk into a new church, they frequently look for something more than a place to worship; they want to experience God's love through community and fellowship. Visitors may feel alone or irrelevant if churchgoers dismiss them or don't provide a warm welcome, which can overshadow any spiritual lessons delivered. To reflect God's love, a church community must be characterized by warmth, friendliness, and hospitality. Without these actions, visitors could find it challenging to connect with the church and, consequently, the love of God that the congregation is supposed to represent.

A welcoming atmosphere demonstrates that the church values every person as a reflection of God's creation. Members who welcome guests, help them feel at home, and show them real interest reflect the acceptance and love that God bestows upon everyone. On the other hand, if members continue to be apathetic or exclusive, it suggests that the church is more concerned with its own membership than with helping others who are in need of support and companionship. This may cause guests to feel ignored and cut off from the message of grace and love they sought when they went. As church members, we have the power and responsibility to actively demonstrate God's love via deliberate acts of hospitality, compassion, and inclusion, empowering us to make a positive impact on others' spiritual experiences.

## NOT FEELING THE LOVE

It comes naturally to people in these societies to engage in conversation and help others feel at ease; in these small exchanges, ties are forged, and strangers are made to feel welcome. I frequently found it more straightforward to converse with foreign strangers than with the folks I encountered regularly while working in Washington, DC. I have lived in Wales, the United Kingdom, and Sicily, Italy. People would converse with strangers in those settings because of a natural openness. That was not the case in Washington, DC, where eye contact was frequently avoided and courteous conversation seemed uncommon. In busy urban settings, when everyone is preoccupied with finding their own way, a disconnect makes essential human connection seem like an afterthought. On the other hand, the willingness to interact with people and the sense of community felt more authentic and natural in countries like Sicily and Wales.

Communicating is just politeness. Commonalities, shared interests, or even generic themes and occurrences are frequently sufficient justifications for doing so. "Good morning" or "good evening" is a simple yet powerful gesture. Comprehending the customs and culture of your community is essential for this. For example, it's considered rude to walk into a room, office, or small business in Italy and give simply a cursory hello. Instead, it is a show of deference to meet each person separately. This small act of personal recognition shows how vital connection and respect are in their culture and emphasizes how much a place's customs may influence how we behave with others.

Acknowledging one another with a nod, a smile, or a simple greeting is often accepted as courteous. When it doesn't, it may seem impolite, but it's usually acceptable because of personal diversions, life's busy schedules, or cultural conventions. Individuals may be distracted, eager to go on to something else, or not used to interacting with strangers. It isn't enjoyable, yet it makes sense in some ways. In a church context, though, the stakes are different. In addition to reflecting Christ's love, the church is supposed to be a haven of fellowship, healing, and community. It can give the impression that the church is more focused on taking care of its own members than on welcoming those who come looking for hope and connection when someone isn't greeted or welcomed.

The first encounter is essential for first-time guests. They can be looking for solace or a sense of community. If you don't acknowledge them, it can make them feel rejected and wonder if the church is a place of love and community. Being courteous isn't enough; showing Christ's love in all you do matters. The church loses a great chance to shine a light on someone who feels invisible or unwelcome after a service. Even in its most basic form, acknowledgment demonstrates the church's concern for, recognition of, and worth for each and every person. It's a modest deed that has a significant impact because it reflects God's heart. Being socially awkward at church doesn't just happen. It's not just rude to avoid interacting with people at church; it's a failure to demonstrate the hospitality and love that characterize a Christian community.

Regretfully, my family and I have personally felt the pain of being abandoned and ignored by a church community. After serving in the armed forces, we were used to relocating every three to four years, which required constant relocation. When we got to our most recent location, we made the decision to attend a denominational church where I had grown up and always felt accepted. But this time, much to our dismay, the experience was very different. We expected to reunite and exchange cordial hellos as we made our way to the back of the church to welcome other guests as they left the service. I was taken aback by the massive influx of people attempting to leave the facility. I had never seen so many people eager to leave the church so quickly; it was like a blue light sale at Kmart or an emergency at their homes. Despite our attempts to establish a connection, we were mainly disregarded, leaving us feeling invisible and unacknowledged.

It was depressing, especially in light of the friendliness and unity I had always connected with that religion. It served as a sad reminder of how a lack of participation may foster an unwelcoming atmosphere that makes newcomers feel alone and unaccepted. These interactions can be depressing and make someone like my family, looking for a sense of belonging, doubt their desire to return. It starkly contrasts the values that a church community ought to uphold: a true sense of love, acceptance, and connection that gives each person a sense of worth and welcome.

# CHAPTER TWO SUMMARY

This chapter examines the concepts of love expressed in the church, spiritual power, and unity, emphasizing how these aspects influence Christians' lives and the success of their mission.

## POWER IN NUMBERS

When people come together in harmony, especially inside the church, there is undeniable power. Scripture frequently emphasizes the value of unity and group power. Ecclesiastes 4:12 writes, "A cord of three strands is not quickly broken," signifying the perseverance that results from working together. This power is embodied in the church, the body of Christ. Together, with a common goal and vision, believers may overcome spiritual obstacles, provide comfort during difficult times, and do far more for God's kingdom than they could on their own. When believers support one another through their faith, prayers, and deeds, they form a more potent force that can withstand physical and spiritual hardships (Stott, 1989).

## THE WHOLE ARMOR OF GOD

The armor of God, described in Ephesians 6:10–18, is typically understood as personal spiritual defense, but when the church dons it, its potency increases. Christians become a cohesive spiritual army instead of solitary fighters when they collectively gird themselves with the sword of the Spirit, the helmet of salvation, the breastplate of righteousness, the belt of truth, and the shield of faith. The church can better spread God's kingdom and withstand the onslaught of the enemy thanks to this armor (Miller, 2008). When the armor is applied collectively, its power is amplified, transforming individual conflicts into group successes. In this sense, the church serves as a battlefield where spiritual victory is achieved by unity in Christ and being a site of worship (Packer, 1993).

## GOD IS LOVE

The fundamental idea of Christianity is that God is love. It is plainly stated in 1 John 4:8, "Whoever does not love does not know God, because God is love." The mission and identity of the church are based on this love. Christians are called to imitate God's unconditional and selfless love in their interpersonal and communal interactions. As a beacon of hope in a broken world, the church is called to mirror this divine love by accepting all individuals and showing compassion (Lowe & Lowe, 2018). The church meets its highest calling when it acts out of love, showing God's love in action by providing material and spiritual help to those in need. The church's strength lies in its numbers and the love that binds those numbers together (Morris, 1981).

## NOT FEELING THE LOVE

Despite the idea of a caring and cohesive church, if people are not welcomed with warmth and concern, they may occasionally feel alone or undesired. A church loses sight of the main reason it exists if it does not show them the love of God. Visitors may feel alienated and unwelcome when members are unkind to them or fail to extend genuine hospitality, which takes away from the message of God's love (Romans 12:10). This stanza encourages everyone to take an active role in fostering an atmosphere where everyone is respected (Bruce, 1984). In addition to impeding spiritual development, a lack of love in the church drives people out of the community and reduces the church's witness to the outside world (Morris, 1981).

In summary, the church's strength is found in its cohesiveness, readiness for spiritual life, and proactive expression of God's love. The church can resist spiritual conflicts and advance God's kingdom by putting all of God's armor together. However, the church also needs to be careful about showing love, making sure that everyone who walks through its doors is made to feel loved and accepted. The church must balance loving community and spiritual power to achieve its mission.

# CHAPTER THREE

# PRAISE

Praise and worship are at the center of church life, which acts as a spiritual conduit between the members and God. These foundational activities ready people's hearts for a closer relationship with God, not just warm-up exercises or parts of a service. Praise strengthens the soul, brings people closer to God, and fosters a sense of togetherness among worshippers. Many people feel the real presence of God during praise and worship when singing, music, and group demonstrations of faith open their hearts. This creates an environment where God's Spirit can flow throughout the congregation and provides a solemn, reverent tone for the service.

Praise in the church may change the atmosphere when it is done with passion, sincerity, and involvement. Attendees' hearts are stirred, and it assists them in turning their attention from the problems of the outside world to God's presence. By using upbeat praise to refocus attention, one can experience breakthroughs in their own lives, a resurgence of faith, and a newfound sense of spiritual vitality. Members of a congregation that experiences dynamic, fervent, and spirit-led praise and worship frequently experience spiritual renewal and a stronger bond with God and one another. This kind of collective worship joins the body of believers in a common encounter with the divine and brings personal fulfillment.

However, there can be a rift between the crowd and the spiritual flow of the service when praise and worship seem flat or uninterested. Lifeless praise can make attendees feel energized and energized. It is typified by halting engagement or robotic repetition. Worship loses its transformational potential when it becomes more of a duty than a sincere act of devotion. Although the congregation members may attend services, their hearts and minds are not involved in worship. This fake disengagement can stifle the spiritual atmosphere and make it more difficult for people to sense God's presence.

The entire service may come across as lifeless or uninteresting when there is a lack of sincerity or intensity during praise and worship. For many churchgoers, these are the times when they feel the closest to God. People's spiritual experience can be weakened by worship that isn't passionate or doesn't engage the congregation, leaving them feeling unfulfilled. Instead of having a profound experience with God, individuals might think they attend a regular event. People may eventually see church attendance as a chore rather than a chance for spiritual rejuvenation if they consistently get uninspired praise. This could result in disengagement or even lead them to quit altogether.

Furthermore, it may be challenging for individuals to engage in a sincere act of praise during worship that is isolated from the assembly. Regardless of a person's spiritual path, worship leaders are essential in fostering an environment in which participation is encouraged. People may find it challenging to participate in worship if it seems impersonal or detached from the crowd. As a result, they may feel more like spectators than active participants. However, when worship is authentic and all-inclusive, the congregation lifts their voices and hearts to God, creating a sense of community.

People are more likely to have a moving spiritual experience that draws them closer to God in congregations where praise and worship are energetic, spirit-filled, and genuine. Worship becomes a moment of genuine connection and introspection because of the praise's vibrant energy. Attendees report feeling more spiritually alive, touched, and rejuvenated after having these experiences. Joyful and passionate praise builds an atmosphere of expectancy where people actively participate in God's worship rather than passively waiting to hear a message. Because of this involvement, people feel motivated, rejuvenated, and prepared to take on life's difficulties with a renewed sense of faith, which fosters individual and group growth.

People could, however, feel let down if the praise is monotonous or lacks vigor as they leave the church. The service may appear dull or unrelated to their spiritual journey if they don't have a strong feeling of spiritual connection. People may gradually stop attending these churches because of this lack of involvement since they may go to other places where they feel more connected during worship. In the end, praise and worship are more than simply songs and instruments; they are vital spiritual rituals that draw the congregation into God's presence. When performed enthusiastically and sincerely, they foster an environment where people's lives are changed, and their hearts are touched.

One of the most amusing yet thought-provoking quotes from the album *Prophetic Music* by well-known preacher A. A. Allen is, "How can you dance to cold dead funeral music?" This insight draws attention to a vital component of spiritual development: happiness and musical expression. Without getting into denominations or their tenets, Christian organizations frequently disagree about music. Historically, some churches have solely used a piano or an organ; hand clapping is not encouraged, raising hands is not encouraged, and dancing is not allowed joyfully or spiritually. Nonetheless, Pentecostal worship customs frequently incorporate tambourines, drums, and animated acts of praise like dancing and clapping. The Bible highlights the importance of music in worship, especially in the Psalms: "Glorify him with dance and timbrels; exalt him with organs and stringed instruments." Praise him with the loud cymbals: Praise him upon the high-sounding cymbals. Let all living things give thanks to the Lord. Give thanks to the Lord" (*King James Version*, 2024, Psalm 150:4-6). This verse favors a livelier style of worship that invites people to show their happiness via song and dance.

Some churches are moving toward more blended worship styles, which reflects the growing desire to create environments where various traditions can coexist. Individual preferences in worship styles continue despite these changes. Some may search for a more exuberant and happier encounter to have a "breakthrough" or be spiritually rejuvenated. Attending such spirited worship sessions gives people a feeling of renewal and fortitude. However, only some are suited for this kind of worship, and it's critical to recognize that spiritual rebirth can take many different forms. It's not required to perform "backflips" during the singing session to go from church with a renewed sense of purpose, a revived viewpoint, and the confidence that one can overcome life's challenges.

## APOTHECARY

The pharmacist had a crucial role in the Tabernacle of Moses by producing the incense and holy anointing oils used in the ritualistic ceremonies. An "apothecary" is a person who combines and makes aromatic or medicinal compounds. Within the Tabernacle, the apothecary's job was to make these holy components in accordance with the guidelines that God gave Moses.

### *The Apothecary's Physical Function*

A thorough explanation of the apothecary's responsibilities may be found in Exodus 30:22–38, when God gave Moses the formula for the incense and holy anointing oil to be used in worship.

Exodus 30:23–24, King James Version: A mixture of pure myrrh, cinnamon, calamus, cassia, and olive oil was to be used to make this oil. Similarly, stacte, onycha, galbanum, and pure frankincense were used to make the incense (Exodus 30:34, KJV).

The anointing oil and incense had practical as well as symbolic significance in the Tabernacle traditions, therefore the apothecary's meticulous preparation of these materials was essential. Exodus 30:26–30 states that the oil was used to anoint the priests and the Tabernacle's furnishings, designating them as holy to the Lord.

According to Psalm 141:2, KJV, the incense burning on the altar symbolized the people's prayers ascending to God. The recipe was strictly followed, which demonstrated respect for the sanctity of the worship ritual.

## *Spiritual Significance of the Apothecary's Work*

The apothecary's physical preparation of the incense and anointing oil is like spiritual acts in modern worship. Today's believers are asked to focused and pure praise and worship, just as the apothecary followed exact instructions to make the sacred oil and incense. The anointing of priests and things with anointing oil represents the anointing of believers with the Holy Spirit. 1 John 2:20, "But you have an unction from the Holy One, and ye know all things" (KJV), alludes to this spiritual anointing. The Tabernacle's actual anointing oil represented God's empowerment and presence, much as believers are empowered in the spiritual world today by the Holy Spirit.

In a similar vein, the incense symbolizes the saints' prayers ascending to God (Revelation 8:3–4, KJV). As a fragrant offering that ascends to God and pleases Him, worship and praise might be thought of as the equivalent of incense in the spiritual world today. The Bible exhorts Christians to "offer the sacrifice of praise to God continually, that is, the fruit of our lips giving thanks to His name" (*King James Version*, 2024, Hebrews 13:15). Just as the pharmacist painstakingly prepared the incense for worship, believers are called to prepare their hearts and minds to provide genuine, heartfelt worship.

## *Worship and Praise as Spiritual Apothecary Practices*

The process of making the holy elements found in the Tabernacle reflects the intentionality required for spiritual activities like praise and worship. As the apothecary painstakingly followed heavenly instructions to make holy oil and incense, so too believers must really adore and worship the Holy Spirit. Like the apothecary physically preparing the sacred components, worship is a spiritual sacramental that needs preparation of the heart as well as singing and other external displays.

In addition, the priests were anointed with oil, signifying their holiness and readiness for divine service. As the Holy Spirit works in the hearts of believers, they are cleansed and set apart for God's service via worship (*King James Version,* 2024, Romans 12:1-2). As a result, the anointing and incense presented in the Tabernacle come to represent how worship and prayer work in the lives of believers, fostering an environment in which God's presence is felt by His people.

In the Tabernacle of Moses, the apothecary played a crucial role in the actual worship ceremonies since they prepared the incense and holy anointing oil precisely and reverently, following the instructions of God. This corresponds to how Christians currently praise and worship in the spiritual domain. Worship and prayer are vital to believers' spiritual life, just as the apothecary's job was necessary for the Israelites' sacred rituals. They represent a fragrant offering and an anointing that calls God into their lives.

## *Being careful as an Apothecary*

The story of Nadab and Abihu, two of Aaron's sons, serves as a sad reminder of the holiness and devotion necessary for worshiping God. Leviticus 10:1-3 tells the story of how Nadab and Abihu sacrificed "unauthorized fire" to the Lord, a rite that resulted in their instantaneous death by heavenly fire.

### The Event: Disobedience in Worship

Among Aaron's four sons, Nadab and Abihu were dedicated as priests and participated extensively in the Tabernacle's priestly functions. The biblical story states that their duty was to present incense, an essential part of worship, and represent the people's prayers ascending to God (Psalm 141:2, New International Version). Nadab and Abihu, the sons of Aaron, took their censers, lit them on fire, and added incense; they then sacrificed illegal fire before the LORD, defying His law, according to Leviticus 10:1 (*New International Version*). The phrase "unauthorized fire" (sometimes translated as "strange fire") implies that they either carried out the ceremonies at an improper time or in an inappropriate way or that they utilized fire that was not taken from the altar as required by Leviticus 16:12. Their acts were a clear transgression of God's directives about how offerings and sacrifices were to be made in the Tabernacle.

## The Consequence: Divine Judgment

According to Leviticus 10:2, NIV, "fire came out from the presence of the Lord and consumed them, and they died before the Lord" in retaliation for their disobedience. This quick and harsh punishment emphasizes regard and obedience to God's worship. It demonstrates how the priests were held to an exceptionally high standard in performing their duties as God's representatives among His people. The fact that God rejected Nadab and Abihu's contribution illustrates how dangerous it is to treat God's holiness improperly.

God's answer also shows that when people behave against His will, even those in positions of spiritual authority are subject to His judgments. Moses gives Aaron the main details of this incident in Leviticus 10:3, where the Lord says, "Among those who approach me I will be proved holy; in the sight of all the people I will be honored" (NIV). This highlights that God's sacredness cannot be undermined or treated carelessly, and that worship is an absolute need.

## Theological Significance

Nadab and Abihu's deaths serve as a reminder that honoring God involves more than merely following rituals; it also entails obedience, reverence, and bringing one's heart into line with what God commands. The "unauthorized fire" signifies a departure from God's explicit instructions, showing that they either took their priestly function lightly or sought to exert their authority over divine instruction. This incident emphasizes a significant topic in the larger framework of Scripture: God's holiness necessitates complete respect and obedience. The instruction to "worship God acceptably with reverence and awe, for our 'God is a consuming fire'" (NIV) in Hebrews 12:28–29 further supports this. Whether worshiping God in the Old Testament or in the present era, one must follow His rules and have a heart that is focused on His glory rather than on one's interests or cultural customs.

## Modern Application

This incident is still significant today, especially in how the church approaches worship. Christians are reminded of the significance of strictly adhering to God's will, just as Nadab and Abihu's disregard for divine commands resulted in their deaths. According to theologian John F. MacArthur (2012), "This incident shows us that not all acts of worship are approved by God. It is necessary to offer worship on His terms, not ours" (p. 58). Churches face the danger of losing sight of the fundamental purpose of worship, which is to present an honest, submissive, and respectful offering to God when their practices become more centered around human preferences or performances.

The narrative of Nadab and Abihu highlights the significance of worshiping God with the appropriate demeanor, deeds, and obedience to His instructions. Their sacrifice of "unauthorized fire" was an act of disobedience that resulted in their death, proving that God's holiness demands the highest regard. The harshness of their punishment serves as a reminder to believers today that worship is more than only performing rituals; it is about seeking God's glory alone and aligning oneself with His will.

# THE DIFFERENCES BETWEEN BIBLICAL PRAISE AND WORSHIP AND MODERN-DAY PRACTICES

Even though praise and worship have been expressed and understood in a variety of ways throughout history and culture, they are still fundamental elements of both biblical and modern Christian practices. The Old and New Testaments provide a wealth of examples of praise and worship, frequently connected to rites, sacrifices, and melodies. On the other hand, due to differences in contemporary practices, denominational views, and cultural influences, there are major differences in modern praise and worship.

## *Biblical Praise and Worship*

Praise and worship in the Old Testament were intimately associated with the sacrifice system and the celebration of religious holidays. During Israel's desert wanderings, worship was mostly gathered at the Tabernacle, and then at the Temple in Jerusalem. Calls to praise abound in the Book of Psalms, frequently conveying delight, respect, and wonder in God.

Psalm 150:3-6, for instance, instructs the people to honor God with trumpets, harps, lyres, tambourines, strings, flutes, and cymbals, among other instruments (New International Version). This kind of acknowledgment was frequently boisterous and joyous, incorporating the entire group in the use of instruments and vocal gestures. Like this, 2 Chronicles 5:13–14 describes the worship at the dedication of Solomon's Temple, when there was a lot of singing and music and God's splendor was so evident that the priests were unable to continue serving (NIV).

Worship evolved into something more spiritual in the New Testament. Jesus, in John 4:23-24, taught that "true worshipers will worship the Father in the Spirit and in truth, for they are the kind of worshipers the Father seeks" (NIV). With the teaching came a change from location-based worship (in the Temple, for example) to an inward, more intimate worship that went beyond actual locations and rituals. In the early church, worship was characterized by the breaking of bread, prayer, teaching, and fellowship in houses where Christians gathered in a more intimate setting, as described in Acts 2:42.

## Modern-Day Praise and Worship

Because of things like culture, technology, and denominational views, the ways that modern Christian's worship have become more varied. The traditional and regimented worship services of the past are being replaced with aspects like multimedia presentations, modern music, and relaxed surroundings in many modern churches. Modern worship bands featuring electric guitars, keyboards, and drums frequently perform during services in many evangelical and Pentecostal churches, resulting in a dynamic and intense atmosphere.

In contrast to the Old Testament's temple-based worship, modern worship is decentralized, with different congregations and denominations using different methods and styles. Certain churches place a strong emphasis on liturgical worship, which is a structured service that includes songs, recitations, and customary rites. Others concentrate on impromptu worship, which encourages a congregation to participate more expressively and emotionally. During the service, this may entail dancing, raising hands, or even making prophecies. All these activities have their roots in biblical customs, but they are frequently modernized and stylized.

Another characteristic of contemporary worship is the focus on one's relationship and personal experience with God. Biblical worship entailed the entire community, while contemporary services—especially those associated with charismatic movements—often emphasize the individual's relationship with God. This is frequently mirrored in the deeply emotional and personal lyrics of modern worship songs, which center on topics like the believer's relationship with God, personal devotion, and God's love (Ingalls et al., 2013).

## *Key Differences*

1. **Location and Rituals**: According to Leviticus 1–7, biblical worship was frequently associated with sites, such as the Tabernacle or Temple, and featured a system of sacrifices and offerings. On the other hand, because it is believed that Jesus completed the duty of sacrifice, modern worship is not limited to a specific physical location and is frequently more casual (Hebrews 9:11–12, NIV).

2. **Music and Instruments**: Psalm 150 describes how a wide range of instruments were frequently used during worship in biblical times. Instruments are still used in

modern worship, but the kinds have changed. In modern churches, electric guitars, synthesizers, and drums are the main musical instruments, however some older churches may still include organs or pianos.

3. **Corporate vs. Individual Focus**: According to 2 Chronicles 5:13–14, NIV, most biblical worship was corporate, involving massive gatherings for festivals, sacrifices, and collective worship. Even while it's still mostly corporate, modern worship frequently emphasizes the value of the individual's experience and relationship with God.

4. **Spontaneity vs. Structure**: Biblical worship, particularly during the Mosaic Law, was very regimented, with God prescribing certain rites and sacrifices (Leviticus 1–7). More spontaneity is allowed in modern worship, especially in charismatic or Pentecostal churches, where worship leaders and attendees may feel inspired to deviate from the schedule to follow the Holy Spirit's guidance.

5. **Theological Understanding**: Worship in the Old Testament was understood as a means of pleasing or honoring God via obedience and sacrifice. Modern worship, on the other hand, emphasizes grace and the relationship between the believer and God, with Jesus viewed as the final sacrifice for sin (Hebrews 9:11–12, NIV). This is especially true in Protestant and evangelical contexts.

The shift from biblical to contemporary worship reflects greater shifts in people's conceptions about their connection with God. While worship in the Bible was closely associated with location and ritual, modern worship is more varied, expressive, and personal, reflecting the many ways that individuals currently engage with their faith. However, the goal of worship is always the same, whether it is in the church now or in ancient Israel: to exalt God and become nearer to His presence.

## ANOINTED PRAISE AND WORSHIP VS. UNANOINTED PRAISE AND WORSHIP

As a means of interaction and communication with God, praise and worship are essential components of the Christian life. However, the spiritual efficacy and genuineness of praise and worship experiences can vary, thus they are not all the same. The Bible states that authentic worship must be done "in spirit and in truth" (New International Version, 2024, John 4:24), which underlines the significance of being guided by the Holy Spirit for worship to be deemed anointed. While unanointed worship lacks this heavenly connection and frequently feels conventional or just performative, anointed praise and worship incorporate a palpable sense of God's presence that moves through worshipers' hearts. As a disclaimer, it's important to note that discernment regarding whether worship is anointed is ultimately a personal judgment for everyone.

### *Anointed Praise and Worship*

The presence and might of the Holy Spirit characterize anointed worship. According to the Bible, "anointing" is a person or object being consecrated or set apart for a divine purpose (Exodus 30:30,

NIV). Anointed worship indicates that the Spirit of God is actively at work in the worship, bringing Christians closer to Him. In addition to exalting God, this kind of worship transforms, heals, and renews people who participate.

An example of anointed worship in the Old Testament is the dedication of Solomon's Temple, where singers and musicians collaborated to exalt God. God's presence was so strong that the priests were unable to carry out their tasks (2 Chronicles 5:13-14, NIV). The reaction demonstrated the anointing: God's glory filled the temple, confirming that He was pleased with the worship that was being offered.

The idea behind contemporary worship is the same. When worship leaders and congregations are tuned in to the Holy Spirit and let Him direct the direction of the service, anointed praise and worship takes place. Freedom in worship, with all the attention on God and not on human performance, is a sign of the anointing. The church consequently has powerful spiritual experiences that include conviction, healing, and a strong sense of God's love and presence. This is consistent with Isaiah 10:27 (NIV), which describes how anointed worship could free people from spiritual oppression by breaking the yokes of bondage.

According to Morris (2003), the strength of anointed worship comes from sincere devotion and a focus on praising God rather than sating congregational expectations or human appetites. The music, words, and actions therefore create a vessel for the Holy Spirit, and the participants themselves become conduits through which God's power flows.

## *Unanointed Praise and Worship*

On the other hand, there is no engagement of the Holy Spirit in unanointed worship. It might be carried out with accuracy and technical mastery, but it lacks the spiritual profundity of anointed worship. People who participate in this type of worship may feel as though they are following a set of rules or rituals rather than developing a genuine relationship with God.

An instance of unanointed worship can be observed in the Old Testament, where God turned away the Israelites' offerings and sacrifices due to their disconnection from Him. According to Isaiah 29:13 (NIV), "These people come near to me with their mouth and honor me with their lips, but their hearts are far from me." This suggests that genuine worship involves an inside, deep commitment to God and goes beyond acts. Worship becomes hollow and ineffectual when there is no genuine spiritual connection.

Worship that isn't anointed frequently prioritizes appearance, fashion, or winning over people over exalting God. This type of worship, according to Tozer (1990), is the outcome of people placing more importance on the structure and form of worship sessions than on the goal of praising God. Even though this kind of worship may be visually or auditorily pleasant, it does not satisfy the spirit, leaving worshippers without a real experience with God.

## Key Differences Between Anointed and Unanointed Worship

1. **Presence of the Holy Spirit**: The Holy Spirit is present during anointed worship, guiding the congregation to a closer relationship with God. Unanointed worship, on the other hand, could seem devoid of any spiritual connection when participants are more preoccupied with outside factors than the actual spiritual act of worship.

2. **God vs. Performance**: Anointed worship places a higher priority on the glorifying of God, with worshipers giving less thought to the service's aesthetics and more thought to pleasing God. On the other side, unanointed worship frequently concentrates on the outward elements, such flawless music, or a spectacular performance, which might divert attention from the real goal of worship.

3. **Transformation and Impact**: People who join in anointed worship experience a transformation in their lives. It can result in healing, spiritual breakthroughs, and a closer bond with God. But because unanointed worship is unable to effect spiritual rebirth, it frequently leaves individuals feeling the same.

4. **Freedom in Worship**: Freedom exists wherever the Lord's Spirit is evident (2 Corinthians 3:17, NIV). Formal boundaries are frequently broken down by anointed worship, enabling people to freely express their adoration by clapping, dancing, singing, and raising of hands. In unanointed worship, people may feel confined or unable to engage fully in the worship experience.

As evidenced by the Bible and contemporary settings, anointed worship is defined by the Holy Spirit's active participation in leading the worshippers into a closer relationship with God. It is characterized by freedom, transformation, and authenticity, all of which support a worship experience that exalts God and fortifies believers' faith. In contrast, unanointed worship may involve technical skill and external performance but lacks the spiritual depth necessary to bring about genuine encounters with God. Because of this, the primary distinction between the two is whether the Holy Spirit is anointed, and this has a profound effect on how worship affects Christians' lives.

# CHAPTER THREE SUMMARY

This chapter delves into the complex concept of praise, examining its spiritual meaning, historical background, and modern church forms. We start by looking at the apothecary's function in the Tabernacle of Moses. The preparation of holy anointing oil and incense for use in worship was the responsibility of the pharmacist, signifying the significance of offerings that make God's nostrils pleased (Exodus 30:22-38, New International Version). This ritual's practical application highlights how our praise and worship must be authentically in line with God's purpose to have a genuine impact, just as proper ingredient preparation is necessary to produce a certain aroma.

Next, we examine the differences between contemporary worship and biblical praise and worship. Biblical praise was frequently performed in groups and involved joyful, jubilant displays of singing, dancing, and instrumental music, as (*New King James Version*, 2024, Psalms 150:4-6) describes. On the other hand, contemporary worship can differ greatly throughout congregations, with some embracing quieter forms of adoration that do not involve the entire body in worship (Goff, 2020). The whole experience of worship may become divided because of this disparity; some people may choose a more contemplative approach, while others may prefer the joyful and inclusive element of biblical praise.

This chapter also discusses the distinction between anointed and unanointed praise and worship. A deeper connection with God results from an authentic Holy Spirit presence during anointed worship (Baird, 2019). It offers a setting where people feel uplifted and spiritually energized. Unanointed praise, on the other hand, could lack this divine presence, seeming more theatrical or robotic and failing to engage the hearts and souls of worshipers (Smith, 2021). Congregations must recognize and foster an atmosphere that is conducive to anointed worship since it has a major effect on the community's spiritual refreshment and progress.

Chapter Three concludes by highlighting the value of comprehending the evolution of praise across time, its historical and spiritual significance, and the fundamental components of an anointed worship experience. The church may cultivate a dynamic community of believers who truly experience God's presence by embracing the rich traditions of biblical praise and incorporating them into modern worship practices.

CHAPTER FOUR

# PREACHING

T he caliber and relevancy of sermons can have a significant
impact on a person's decision to stay in church or not. As a
source of guidance and inspiration for the congregation, sermons
are essential to spiritual development and fostering a sense of
community. A well-written sermon should be grounded in solid
scriptural teachings and presented in a way that draws the audience
in and addresses their practical issues while providing biblical
insight. Preachers must make the connection between scripture
and the pleasures, sorrows, and difficulties that their congregation
faces on a daily basis because the sermon serves as a bridge between
timeless principles and contemporary application. Failure to do so
can lead to a disengaged congregation and a weakened sense of
community.

Sermons can captivate audiences and inspire more in-depth
thought and action when they are pertinent to their individual
and group experiences. Sermons tackling real-life issues, such as
faith, family, finances, or personal development, enable attendees

to understand better how the Bible's lessons relate to their lives. Because of its applicability, the message feels honest, approachable, and practical. When sermons touch on practical issues and provide spiritual direction that makes life easier, people are more likely to remain interested and keep coming. A sermon that strikes a deep chord with the audience has the power to transform, opening their minds to fresh ideas and enhancing their bond with God.

Furthermore, engaging sermons challenge and elicit thought in addition to providing information. They inspire people to consider their attitudes, actions, and beliefs in the context of scripture, which leads to a more profound connection with their faith. Sermons that challenge listeners' preconceived notions and encourage critical thinking encourage them to engage with theological issues, reflect on their religious practices, and act toward their spiritual and personal development. These provocative teachings contribute to developing a culture where faith is dynamic, ever-expanding, and dynamic.

Sermons that lack depth or sophistication, on the other hand, can alienate and repel their audience. A sermon that lacks depth may not be able to retain the congregation's interest or provide much spiritual food, either because it is straightforward or ignores the complexity of scripture and life. Sermons that follow a conventional pattern or do not provide novel perspectives can come across as dull and monotonous, which may lead the audience to lose interest or, in certain situations, look for spiritual solace elsewhere.

There is even more competition for a church's message to be seen in the modern world of abundant spiritual resources available online. People may become less motivated to attend sermons if they do not provide something of value—something that challenges the listener, establishes a connection with God, and equips them for everyday life. Instead, they can look for sermons online or at different churches where they feel more intellectually and spiritually fulfilled. This highlights the need for sermons to be engaging and valuable in order to retain their audience.

Thus, the secret to effective preaching is imparting biblical facts in a way that engages the audience intellectually, emotionally, and spiritually. An effective sermon may uplift, challenge, inspire, and transform people, bringing them closer to God and bolstering the church body. On the other hand, a dull lecture has the potential to turn people away, demotivating them to come back.

Preaching is a subject that frequently sparks disagreement and discussion in religious communities. Usually, when one thinks of a preacher, they picture a person behind a pulpit—someone who has completed formal schooling in a seminary or been ordained to preach in a particular church setting. This conventional viewpoint creates a distinct line between those who are permitted to preach and those who are not, reinforcing the notion that preaching is only for those who have obtained specific training and recognition.

Preaching, however, has dynamics that go beyond the speaker's credentials. A sermon's influence and efficacy can also be greatly influenced by the setting in which it is given and the spiritual condition of the audience. Preaching has a subjective component, much as there is a range of judgments regarding what defines "anointed" praise and worship. Different people will respond differently to a message that strikes them as a potent, Spirit-led message; hence, perspectives of the preaching's authenticity and quality may differ.

Significant queries concerning the nature of preaching itself are brought up by this variability. Does the success of the message depend just on the credentials of the speaker, or does it also heavily depend on the environment, the openness of the congregation, and the leading of the Holy Spirit? This intricacy invites listeners to exercise judgment and introspection, taking into account not only the style of delivery of the sermon but also its consistency with biblical teachings and application to their personal spiritual development.

Preaching is essentially a complex topic that requires both pastors and followers to traverse their own conceptions of power, anointing, and the community's spiritual demands. Accepting this complexity can result in more in-depth conversations regarding the nature of preaching and its essential function in the church's existence, which will ultimately help to create an atmosphere in which all members are encouraged to share their faith and make a positive impact on the body of Christ.

## BISHOP MICHAEL PITTS

"Lines have become so blurred so much that preachers looking like motivational speakers  and motivational speakers trying to look like preachers," Bishop Michael Pitts (Gospel Classroom for All Nation, 2023) remarked perceptively. This claim captures a dramatic change in the field of preaching as well as the larger picture of church leadership. The line between motivational speaking and preaching has blurred more and more in modern contexts.

Many contemporary preachers have embraced the methods and approaches frequently used by motivational speakers, placing more emphasis on charisma, stage presence, and personal tales than on the conventional, theologically based sermon delivery. This blurring of roles calls into question the fundamental nature and function of preaching within the context of the church. While motivational speakers seek to uplift and motivate audiences toward personal development and goals, preachers' main objectives are to share God's Word, challenge Christians to grow in their faith, and promote a closer bond with Christ.

The message may be diluted when motivational speaking tactics are used in sermons. Catchy phrases or upbeat anecdotes run the risk of overshadowing the profound truths of Scripture when the emphasis switches to entertainment value or audience involvement. While it is crucial to engage with congregants and communicate ideas in a sympathetic manner, the basic message should remain founded in biblical teachings and theological truths.

Furthermore, this tendency could encourage a shallow culture among churchgoers. Rather than being encouraged to consider their spiritual lives, confess their sins, and work toward a sincere connection with God, congregations may grow accustomed to feel-good sermons that satisfy their whims. Fostering a community that prioritizes emotional highs over life-changing experiences with the Holy Spirit carries a risk.

This change means that both church leaders and members need to be able to distinguish between a sermon that inspires and one that edifies. A more genuine worship and fellowship experience inside the church can result from encouraging preachers to stay rooted in Scripture while delivering teachings that inspire and encourage. In the end, it's critical to understand that a preacher's job description goes beyond mere amusement; it is a holy duty to share the gospel truth and mentor Christians on their spiritual paths.

## CALLED FOR A SEASON?

Within Christian circles, there is a great deal of controversy over whether preaching is a temporary calling or a lifetime vocation. Many people have a calling to ministry at an early age, but they may decide to postpone fully dedicating themselves to preaching and working in the church until they are older and more established. There are several reasons for this delayed response, such as personal circumstances, academic goals, or a desire to acquire life experience prior to assuming such a large role.

Some people believe that a preacher must be completely committed to the ministry from the beginning and that the calling to preach is a lifetime responsibility. Nevertheless, this viewpoint might overlook the various means by which God might mold people into capable ministers. As indicated in 1 Timothy 4:14 (New International Version), Paul encourages Timothy to "not neglect your gift, which was given you through prophecy when the body of elders laid their hands on you." This suggests that a person's calling may change over time and not always call for a full-time commitment right once.

Furthermore, there are many who preach without receiving full-time assistance from the ministry. These lay preachers frequently work additional jobs and make major contributions to their churches. Their distinct experiences can add depth to their sermons, offering relatable perspectives that strike a chord with their audiences. It is stressed in 1 Peter 4:10–11 (NIV) that all believers, regardless of their full-time status, should use whatever gift they have been given to help others, including preaching.

In conclusion, the call to preach does not always need a lifetime of commitment. It can take many different forms. People may find their calling at different times in their lives and serve in different capacities, either full-time or on a part-time basis. Preaching is most effective when the preacher is sincere in their heart and is prepared to follow God's direction no matter how long they have been in ministry.

## Knowing When to Stop

The mere fact that someone is not physically present in the "pulpit" does not take away from their calling or capacity to preach the gospel. Since sharing the Gospel and announcing the truths of Scripture are at the core of preaching, its reach is not limited to conventional church settings.

Scripture has examples of people who were meant for jobs or periods of time. For instance, the apostle Paul's missionary travels, whose main objective was to preach the gospel to Gentiles, significantly contributed to the early church's expansion (Acts 9:15). Nevertheless, Paul recognized the necessity of change and periodically departed from churches or areas to allow space for new leaders or to focus on other ministries (Acts 16:6–10). This illustrates how a ministry can be dynamic and how a calling can involve multiple stages.

The apostle Paul also underlined that the gospel's reach is unconstrained by geography or official status. He admits in Philippians 1:15–18 (NIV) that while some preach Christ sincerely, others do so out of jealousy or other ill intent. Finally, he says, "But what difference does it make? Whether the intentions are true or not, what counts is that Christ is preached in every way. This demonstrates that the main emphasis should remain on the presentation of Christ rather than the setting in which it occurs.

Furthermore, people may function as conduits for God's Word in their daily lives by sharing the message via deeds and conversations. According to Jesus, believers are "the light of the world," and he exhorts them to let their light show before others in Matthew 5:14–16 (NIV). This indicates that one can preach by genuinely practicing their faith and having an impact on others by service, love, and testimony.

Preaching, at its core, is about delivering the good news of Jesus Christ and making disciples, regardless of platform; it is about more than just the pulpit. Matthew 28:19–20 (NIV), the Great Commission, reminds Christians of their duty to "go and make disciples of all nations," highlighting the fact that ministry can take place anywhere and is not limited to a conventional preaching setting.

In conclusion, even though preaching has traditionally taken place in the pulpit, sharing the gospel is not limited to that area. Christians can preach the Bible in a variety of settings, proving that their ministry and witness may have a big impact both inside and outside of their communities.

## CALLED OR JUST WENT?

A major theme running through the Bible is that of being "called" to preach, signifying that certain functions within the church are assigned to people by divine appointment. God has assigned the church many duties, such as apostles, prophets, evangelists, pastors, and teachers, in Ephesians 4:11–12 (New International Version), with the aim of strengthening the church and empowering the saints. According to this, a true calling entails more than just personal aspiration; it also calls for heavenly confirmation and a sense of purpose that is in line with God's purposes for the church.

On the other hand, some people nowadays might decide to pursue a career in preaching even when they do not feel a strong sense of a divine calling. Important concerns about the reasons underlying these judgments are brought up by this phenomenon. Instead of accepting God's invitation, some people may choose to become preachers to achieve personal fulfillment, elevate their social standing, or increase their income. While their intentions may be sincere, the lack of a genuine calling can lead to challenges in their ministry, such as spiritual burnout, lack of effectiveness, or failure to connect with their congregations.

The Bible contains countless examples of persons who were called by God to serve in ministry. For example, Jeremiah was designated as a prophet even before his birth (Jeremiah 1:5), and Moses was asked to lead the Israelites out of Egypt (Exodus 3:10). These biblical characters demonstrated a strong sense of purpose and dedication in response to God's call.

Furthermore, the New Testament places a strong emphasis on the value of spiritual discernment in identifying one's vocation.

Paul discusses the many duties and gifts within the church in Romans 12:6–8 (NIV), exhorting Christians to use their gifts in accordance with the grace bestowed upon them. This emphasizes how important it is for people to pray, study the Bible, and speak with experienced Christians to seek God's direction before deciding whether to serve in ministry.

In conclusion, the biblical view of calling highlights that preaching is a divine appointment that necessitates careful judgment and obedience rather than just being a career or a human choice. Even though some people may begin the ministry without having a clear calling, their service's efficacy and sustainability could be jeopardized if they don't have the basis of a legitimate divine commission.

## MILK OR MEAT

Effective ministry requires an understanding of the audience being preached to, particularly when assisting people in transitioning from youthful to mature Christianity. The Bible places a strong emphasis on communicating ideas that are relevant to listeners at different points in their spiritual journey. The New International Version (NIV) of 1 Corinthians 3:2 quotes Paul as saying, "I gave you milk, not solid food, because you were not yet ready for it." This analogy highlights the necessity of providing spiritual care that is appropriate for the congregation's stage of development. Similar to how a newborn is weaned off of solid food and then given milk, so too do new converts need to be taught the fundamentals before they can understand more advanced theological ideas.

Sermons ought to be inclusive and enlightening, catering to the various stages of spiritual development within the congregation. According to Ephesians 4:11-13 (NIV), the Lord "gave some to be apostles, some prophets, some evangelists, and some pastors and teachers, to prepare God's people for works of service, so that the body of Christ may be built up until we all reach unity in the faith." This verse makes clear that church leaders have specific responsibilities to support the growth and development of all believers, regardless of their level of spiritual maturity.

To guarantee that the message is understood and connected with by all members of the congregation, a preacher must speak with great attention. Communication must be designed to guide and educate both new converts and seasoned Christians, offering guidance and fundamental understanding to both groups. Jesus Himself served as an example of this strategy, frequently instructing through parables (Matthew 13:34, NIV). He was able to convey important lessons in a way that was understandable to everyone by using parables to convey difficult ideas.

Preachers also need to be aware of the social and cultural backgrounds of their audience. Paul's well-known speech on Mars Hill, found in Acts 17:22–34, is a perfect example of how knowing your audience may influence the message. Paul made use of Greek poetry, culture, and religion when speaking to Greek philosophers in order to make his point about Christ approachable and comprehensible. Nowadays, preaching calls for a same level of cultural sensitivity and awareness.

To stimulate growth in every believer, a sermon must provide something for everyone. According to 2 Timothy 3:16-17 (NIV),

"All Scripture is God-breathed and is useful for teaching, rebuking, correcting, and training in righteousness, so that the servant of God may be thoroughly equipped for every good work." The message should encourage young Christians in their newfound faith, while challenging mature believers to go deeper in their understanding and walk with God.

A preacher's ability to comprehend the spiritual development and cultural background of their audience determines how effective their sermons will be. By meticulously structuring messages and assuring clarity, preachers can provide sermons that not only nurture new believers but also edify seasoned Christians, ensuring that all receive a portion of the message that speaks to them.

Because they lack theological depth or skill, some preachers may find themselves providing more of what the Apostle Paul calls "milk" than "solid food" in their sermons. The New International Version (NIV) of 1 Corinthians 3:2 quotes Paul as saying, "I gave you milk, not solid food, because you were not yet ready for it." This analogy emphasizes how important it is to give newer Christians who are still developing their religion basic, understandable lessons. But preachers who are not well-versed in scriptural interpretation and Scripture may inadvertently limit themselves to these basic lessons. These preachers run the danger of misunderstandings or confusion when they try to dive into more difficult subjects like exegesis and hermeneutics without having the necessary training or preparation.

Hermeneutics, the theory and practice of text interpretation, and exegesis, the critical explanation or interpretation of a biblical text, are essential tools for a greater knowledge of Scripture

(Osborne, 2006). But these call for a certain amount of knowledge, study, and training in theology. Preachers who try to dissect these issues without the necessary expertise risk misquoting Scripture or oversimplifying difficult theological themes. As a result, while presenting biblical facts, they can come across as unprepared or even silly.

The apostle James issues a sobering caution in James 3:1 (NIV): "My fellow believers, not many of you should become teachers because you know that we who teach will be judged more strictly." The task of teaching God's Word is extremely serious. Inadequate preparation or comprehension can result in mishandling Scripture, which can cause confusion in the congregation, spiritual stagnation, or even misdirection. An insufficient or erroneous understanding of Scripture may hinder the spiritual development of individuals who are ready to learn, rather than strengthening the congregation's faith.

Some preachers may feel compelled to address difficult theological subjects because of their sincere love for God and desire to share His Word, but if they are not well-prepared, their sermons may fall flat. Preachers need to understand that their duty extends beyond simply imparting knowledge; it also includes making sure that the information is sound biblically and spiritually. "Do your best to present yourself to God as one approved, a worker who does not need to be ashamed and who correctly handles the word of truth" (2 Timothy 2:15, NIV) is a timeless piece of advice from Paul to Timothy.

Preachers can benefit from theological education, mentorship, and ongoing Word study in order to avoid making the mistake of preaching sermons that are either superficial or ignorant. While it is not expected of a preacher to be an expert in everything, admitting one's limitations and making the commitment to lifelong learning do need a certain humility and discipline. In addition to displaying a strong faith, preaching need also exhibit sound doctrine and a conscientious commitment to scriptural interpretation.

Finally, it should be noted that although it is crucial for pastors to assist their flocks in transitioning from spiritual "milk" to "solid food," they also need to make sure they have the knowledge and resources necessary to accomplish this. Without the necessary knowledge, attempting to dissect exegesis and hermeneutics can lead to misunderstandings and, occasionally, absurdity. Preachers ought to study Scripture with diligence, understanding that the task of teaching entails a heavy load that needs to be fulfilled with careful planning.

## KEEPING PEOPLE WITH PREACHING

Traditionally, preaching has been used to promote spiritual development and to bring people closer to God. Preaching, however, occasionally unintentionally drives individuals away from the church. This might happen for several reasons, such as the content of the message, the method of delivery, or the perceived attitude of the preacher. Instead of bringing people closer to God, a message that is unduly judgmental, uncaring, or does not speak to the needs of the congregation may drive them away.

## *Content of the Message*

The content of the sermon itself is one of the main ways that preaching can discourage people from attending church. Sermons that place an excessive amount of emphasis on condemnation without providing grace or doable solutions for people's everyday problems may make listeners feel condemned rather than encouraged. Many people quit church because they think it's too harsh or unimportant, according to Barna (2018). Preaching that prioritizes love and redemption over sin and punishment can be divisive, particularly for individuals who are already experiencing feelings of guilt or inadequacy. Disengagement might result from messages that don't speak to the congregation's actual issues because they look out of touch.

## *Delivery and Style*

The way a sermon is delivered can also affect whether or not listeners feel accepted or alienated. Overly cerebral or theologically technical preaching has the potential to confuse rather than to inspire. Effective preaching, according to Keller (2015), must be understandable and approachable to the audience in order to avoid alienating individuals who lack in-depth biblical understanding. On the other hand, preaching that is overly straightforward or neglects to address more profound spiritual realities may make mature Christians feel unsupported and encourage them to look elsewhere for deeper and more meaningful interaction.

Furthermore, a tone that is authoritative or sanctimonious may turn people off. According to Pew Research (2016), a lot of people give up going to church because they think religious leaders are conceited or hypocritical. Preachers run the risk of establishing an environment that feels judgmental and restrictive when they take on a superior attitude and speak down to the congregation rather than encouraging an inclusive and humble discussion.

## The Importance of Compassion and Relevance

People can also be turned off by sermons that lack empathy and don't address the congregation's problems. In one-on-one conversations as well as from the pulpit, pastoral care is crucial. People may feel cut off from the sermon and the church if the speaker does not show empathy for the suffering and difficulties of the listeners. Chan (2016) asserts that preaching ought to be a loving deed motivated by compassion and a desire to uphold the listeners' faith. Instead, then concentrating only on theoretical ideas, sermons that provide hope and real-world application enable listeners to develop a deeper relationship with their faith and the church.

Although the purpose of preaching is to edify and uplift, it may also alienate people if it is given in a way that is inconsiderate of their needs and spiritual growth. Disengagement with the church can be caused by judgmental messages, unclear or oversimplified material, and an unwelcoming delivery style. Compassion, grace, and relevancy are the foundations of effective preaching, which guarantees that the message not only strikes a chord but also fosters the congregation's faith and general well-being.

# CHAPTER FOUR SUMMARY

The nature of pastoral calling, the complexities of preaching, and the impact of sermon content on congregations are all examined in this chapter. Bishop Pitts' criticism that preachers today sometimes resemble motivational speakers, blurring the borders between spiritual calling and secular performance, is the starting point for discussion. This insight establishes the framework for a discussion of what it means to be properly "called" to preach and whether or not that calling is cyclical.

Being "called for a season" highlights the fact that not all preaching missions are long-term. Before moving on to other facets of ministry or quitting completely, some ministers may be called to serve for a set period of time, goal, or season in their lives. This casts doubt on the idea that a preacher's divine calling can only be fulfilled by spending their entire life in the pulpit. Recognizing that God's timing might not always line up with human expectations, humility and discernment in service are made possible by an understanding of the ebb and flow of a spiritual calling.

The chapter also explores the biblical "Milk or Meat" comparison (1 Corinthians 3:1–3; Hebrews 5:12–14), which compares spiritual lessons to sustenance. Some preachers may only provide "milk"—basic, readily understood teachings—when the congregation is ready for "meat," or deeper spiritual truths. This could be due to a lack of theological experience or depth. This disparity can cause new believers to feel disenchanted if the message is overly complicated, while spiritually mature members of the congregation who long for a deeper knowledge may get frustrated. Preaching must be balanced in order to meet the requirements of all listeners, regardless of their level of spiritual development.

Lastly, the chapter addresses how preaching has the power to draw people to the church or drive them away. Sermons with an emphasis on grace, love, and useful application tend to draw listeners in, whereas sermons that are unduly critical, irrelevant, or callous tend to turn people off. Sermon content, tone, and style all have a big influence on whether or not attendees feel accepted and a part of the church. In this section, the significance of preachers knowing their audience and tailoring sermons to meet the needs of a diverse congregation—whether through "milk" or "meat" teachings—is emphasized.

## Key Points

- Bishop Michael Pitts highlights the peril of forgoing the depth of a spiritual calling in favor of showbiz when he observes that preachers frequently sound like motivational speakers.
- The idea of being "called for a season" challenges the conventional notion of lifelong ministry by highlighting discernment and humility in following God's call.
- The "Milk or Meat" analogy highlights the importance of delivering messages that cater to both new and mature believers, ensuring spiritual growth for everyone.
- Preaching places a strong emphasis on the importance of empathy and sermon relevance. Preaching has the power to either draw people closer to God or drive them away, depending on its substance, tone, and delivery.

# CHAPTER FIVE

# SUMMARIZATION OF THE 4 P'S

More than twenty years ago, it became clear to me why so many people leave churches when one or more of the "4 Ps"—Place, People, Praise, and Preaching—are absent or insufficient. In addition to being fundamental pillars, these "4 Ps" serve as the cornerstone for creating an environment where individuals feel involved, connected, and spiritually nourished. When any of these elements are absent or insufficient, it has a substantial effect on the experience of attendees, which often results in disengagement and, eventually, a drop in attendance. It's critical to comprehend the grave repercussions of ignoring these "4 Ps."

## Place

A church's material and spiritual surroundings significantly impact how long its members stay. It goes beyond aesthetics to make a room inviting, cozy, and suitable for worship. According to Rainer (2013), a church should offer a haven from the stresses of everyday life, where individuals can feel secure and a part of something bigger than themselves. People are less likely to return when the "place" is chilly, disorganized, or unwelcoming because they don't feel like they belong or are in God's presence.

## People

A church's sense of community is essential. Empirical studies have demonstrated that a critical factor driving individuals to attend church again is a sense of community (Dudley & Roizen, 2001). A hospitable, encouraging, and inclusive church creates a strong feeling of community. Members are less inclined to stick around if they feel alone, criticized, or disregarded. Relationships and fellowship are essential to church life because they make people feel important and a part of the more prominent church family (Acts 2:42, NIV). In the absence of these ties, disengagement is nearly inevitable.

## Praise

Worship and praise are essential parts of religious services. They uplift the soul and bring individuals nearer to God (Psalm 100:2-4, NIV). However, praise detracts from the worship experience if it seems uninspired or disengaged from the assembly. Bright and sincere praise, according to Noland (2009), draws individuals into God's presence and promotes a closer spiritual bond. Members may become bored and dissatisfied with worship and stop coming to services if it is routine or lacking passion.

## Preaching

Ultimately, whether a person leaves a church is mainly determined by the caliber of the sermons. People are drawn in and encouraged to grow spiritually when preaching is firmly grounded in Scripture and applicable to the congregation's lives (2 Timothy 4:2, NIV). Conversely, sermons that lack depth, originality, or relevance can turn off listeners because they don't provoke thought or challenge them. Preaching should encourage intellectual engagement with the gospel and encourage listeners to apply biblical principles to their everyday lives, as suggested by Keller (2015). If sermons fail to do this, people lose interest and finally quit attending church.

In conclusion, the '4 Ps'—Place, People, Praise, and Preaching— are not only elements; rather, they represent the core of a church environment that cultivates a deep feeling of community and spiritual fulfillment. When any of these components are missing or inadequate, people may become alienated and church attendance may decrease. By attending to these elements and creating an environment that encourages worship, fellowship, and spiritual development, churches cannot only increase attendance but also provide each visitor with a deeply memorable and spiritually fulfilling experience.

# REFERENCES

*1 Chronicles 4 NIV.* (2024). Biblehub.com. https://biblehub.com/niv/1_chronicles/4.htm

*1 Chronicles 6 NIV.* (2024). Biblehub.com. https://biblehub.com/niv/1_chronicles/6.htm

*1 Chronicles 15 NIV.* (2024). Biblehub.com. https://biblehub.com/niv/1_chronicles/15.htm

*1 Chronicles 16 NIV.* (2024). Biblehub.com. https://biblehub.com/niv/1_chronicles/16.htm

*1 Corinthians 3 NIV.* (2024). Biblehub.com. https://biblehub.com/niv/1_corinthians/3.htm

*1 John 4 KJV.* (n.d.). Biblehub.com. https://biblehub.com/kjv/1_john/4.htm

*1 Kings 6 NIV.* (2024). Biblehub.com. https://biblehub.com/niv/2_chronicles/6.htm

*1 Kings 7 NIV.* (2024). Biblehub.com. https://biblehub.com/niv/2_chronicles/7.htm

*1 Peter 4 NIV.* (2024). Biblehub.com. https://biblehub.com/niv/1_peter/4.htm

*1 Thessalonians 5 NIV.* (2024). Biblehub.com. https://biblehub.com/niv/1_thessalonians/5.htm

*2 Chronicles 3 NIV.* (2024). Biblehub.com. https://biblehub.com/niv/2_chronicles/3.htm

*2 Chronicles 3 NIV.* (2024). Biblehub.com. https://biblehub.com/niv/2_chronicles/3.htm

*2 Chronicles 5 NIV.* (2024). Biblehub.com. https://biblehub.com/niv/2_chronicles/5.htm

*2 Corinthians 3 NIV.* (2024). Biblehub.com. https://biblehub.com/niv/2_corinthians/3.htm

*2 Kings 25 NIV.* (2024). Biblehub.com. https://biblehub.com/niv/2_kings/25.htm

*2 Samuel 7 NIV.* (2024). Biblehub.com. https://biblehub.com/niv/2_samuel/7.htm

*2 Samuel 6 NIV.* (2024). Biblehub.com. https://biblehub.com/niv/2_samuel/6.htm

*2 Timothy 2 NIV.* (2024). Biblehub.com. https://biblehub.com/niv/2_timothy/2.htm

*2 Timothy 3 NIV*. (2024). Biblehub.com. https://biblehub.com/niv/2_timothy/3.htm

*2 Timothy 4 NIV*. (2024). Biblehub.com. https://biblehub.com/niv/2_timothy/4.htm

*Acts 1 NIV*. (2024). Biblehub.com. https://biblehub.com/niv/acts/1.htm

*Acts 2 NIV*. (2024). Biblehub.com. https://biblehub.com/niv/acts/2.htm

*Acts 9 NIV*. (2024). Biblehub.com. https://biblehub.com/niv/acts/9.htm

*Acts 13 NIV*. (2024). Biblehub.com. https://biblehub.com/niv/acts/13.htm

*Acts 16 NIV*. (2024). Biblehub.com. https://biblehub.com/niv/acts/16.htm

*Acts 17 NIV*. (2024). Biblehub.com. https://biblehub.com/niv/acts/17.htm

Ammerman, N. T. (2013). *Congregations in America*. Harvard University Press.

Baird, T. (2019). *Worship in spirit and truth: Understanding anointed praise*. Faith Press.

Ball, S. (2020). *15 reasons why committed Christians do not attend church*. The Malphurs Group. Retrieved from https://malphursgroup.com/15-reasons-why-committed-christians-do-not-attend-church/

Barna Group. (2018). *The state of the church 2018*. Barna Group.

Bruce, F. F. (1984). *The epistle to the Romans*. Eerdmans Publishing.

Chan, F. (2016). *Preaching and teaching with imagination*. David C. Cook.

*Deuteronomy 12 NIV*. (2024). Biblehub.com. https://biblehub.com/niv/deuteronomy/12.htm

Dudley, C. S., & Roizen, D. A. (2001). *Faith communities today: A report on religion in the United States today*. Hartford Institute for Religion Research.

*Ephesians 4 NIV*. (2024). Biblehub.com. https://biblehub.com/niv/ephesians/4.htm

*Ephesians 6 NIV*. (2024). Biblehub.com. https://biblehub.com/niv/ephesians/6.htm

*Exodus 3 NIV*. (2024). Biblehub.com. https://biblehub.com/niv/exodus/3.htm

*Exodus 25 NIV*. (2024). Biblehub.com. https://biblehub.com/niv/exodus/25.htm

*Exodus 26 NIV.* (2024). Biblehub.com. https://biblehub.com/niv/exodus/26.htm

*Exodus 27 NIV.* (2024). Biblehub.com. https://biblehub.com/niv/exodus/27.htm

*Exodus 30 NIV.* (2024). Biblehub.com. https://biblehub.com/niv/exodus/30.htm

*Exodus 30 KJV.* (2024). Biblehub.com. https://biblehub.com/kjv/exodus/30.htm

*Ezekiel 8 NIV.* (2024). Biblehub.com. https://biblehub.com/niv/ezekiel/8.htm

*Ezra 1 NIV.* (2024). Biblehub.com. https://biblehub.com/niv/ezra/1.htm

Ferguson, E. (1999). *The Church of Christ: A Biblical Ecclesiology for Today.* Wipf and Stock Publishers.

Ferguson, E. (2013). *Church history: From Christ to pre-reformation.* Zondervan.

Goff, M. (2020). *Worship across the ages: A comparative study of Biblical and modern practices.* Theological Studies Journal, 45(3), 221-234.

Gospel Classroom for All Nation. (2023, July 31). *The situation of #church in 1997 Azusa Street.* Grace TV. [YouTube]. https://www.youtube.com/watch?v=zTevo_4Q0bY

*Hebrews 5 NIV.* (2024). Biblehub.com. https://biblehub.com/niv/hebrews/5.htm

*Hebrews 9 NIV.* (2024). Biblehub.com. https://biblehub.com/niv/hebrews/9.htm

*Hebrews 12 NIV.* (2024). Biblehub.com. https://biblehub.com/niv/hebrews/12.htm

*Hebrews 13 NKJV.* (2024). Biblehub.com. https://biblehub.com/nkjv/hebrews/13.htm

Ingalls, M. M., Yong, A., & Wagner, T. (2013). *The Spirit of praise: Music and worship in global Pentecostal-charismatic Christianity.* Penn State Press.

IN. (2023, July 31). *Michael Pitts Jun. THE SITUATION OF #CHURCH IN 1997 AZUSA STREET.GRACE TV.SUBSCRIBE TO GET GOOD NEWS.* YouTube. https://youtu.be/zTevo_4Q0bY?si=uvj4p3nqqVGpTSkF

*Isaiah 29 NIV.* (2024). Biblehub.com. https://biblehub.com/niv/isaiah/29.htm

*James 3 NIV. (2024).* Biblehub.com. https://biblehub.com/niv/james/3.htm

*Jeremiah 1 NIV.* (2024). Biblehub.com. https://biblehub.com/niv/jeremiah/1.htm

*John 4 NIV.* (2024). Biblehub.com. https://biblehub.com/niv/john/4.htm

Josephus, F. (1981). *The Antiquities of the Jews* (H. St. J. Thackeray, Trans.). Harvard University Press.

Keller, T. (2015). *Preaching: Communicating faith in an age of skepticism.* Viking

Kilde, J. H. (2008). Sacred power, sacred space: An introduction to Christian architecture and worship. Oxford University Pre

*King James Bible* (2024). Bible Hub. Psalm 150 KJV (biblehub.com)

Lee, M. A. (2014). Synagogue: An Analysis of Its Role in Jewish Society. *Journal of Jewish Studies, 65*(1), 45-63.

*Leviticus 10 NIV.* (2024). Biblehub.com. https://biblehub.com/niv/leviticus/10.htm

*Leviticus 16 NIV.* (2024). Biblehub.com. https://biblehub.com/niv/leviticus/16.htm

Lowe, W. & Lowe, R. (2018). *Access through Christ: The connection of believers.* Ministry Publishing.

*Luke 4 NIV.* (2024). Biblehub.com. https://biblehub.com/niv/luke/4.htm

MacArthur, J. F. (2012). *Strange Fire: The danger of offending the Holy Spirit with counterfeit worship*. Nashville: Thomas Nelson.

*Matthew 4 NIV*. (2024). Biblehub.com. https://biblehub.com/niv/matthew/4.htm

*Matthew 5 NIV*. (2024). Biblehub.com. https://biblehub.com/niv/matthew/5.htm

*Matthew 13 NIV*. (2024). Biblehub.com. https://biblehub.com/niv/matthew/13.htm

*Matthew 28 NIV*. (2024). Biblehub.com. https://biblehub.com/niv/matthew/28.htm

*Mark 1 NIV*. (2024). Biblehub.com. https://biblehub.com/niv/mark/1.htm

Merrill, E. H. (2000). *An Historical Theology of the Tabernacle: The Tabernacle and the*

Miller, D. (2008). *Spiritual Warfare: The Corporate Armor of God*. FaithWorks Publishing.

Morris, L. (1981). *The first epistle of John: Revised edition*. Eerdmans Publishing.

Morris, R. (2003). *The power of praise and worship*. Thomas Nelson.

*Nehemiah 8 NIV*. (2024). Biblehub.com. https://biblehub.com/niv/nehemiah/8.htm

Noland, R. (2009). *The heart of the artist: A character-building guide for you and your ministry team.* Zondervan

Osborne, G. R. (2006). *The hermeneutical spiral: A comprehensive introduction to biblical interpretation* (Rev. ed.). InterVarsity Press.

Packer, J. I. (1993). *Knowing God.* IVP Books

Pew Research Center. (2016). *Why Americans go (and don't go) to religious services.* Pew Research Center.

*Philippians 1 NIV*. (2024.). Biblehub.com. https://biblehub.com/niv/philippians/1.htm

*Psalm 100 NIV*. (2024). Biblehub.com. https://biblehub.com/niv/psalms/100.htm

*Psalm 150 KJV*. (2024). Biblehub.com. https://biblehub.com/kjv/psalms/150.htm

*Psalm 150 NKJV*. (2024). Biblehub.com. https://biblehub.com/nkjv/psalms/150.htm

Rainer, T. S. (2013). *I am a church member: Discovering the attitude that makes the difference.* B&H Publishing Group.

*Revelation 8 NKJV.* (2024). Biblehub.com. https://biblehub.com/nkjv/revelation/8.htm

*Romans 12 NKJV.* (2024). Biblehub.com. https://biblehub.com/nkjv/romans/12.htm

*Romans 12 NIV.* (2024). Biblehub.com. https://biblehub.com/niv/romans/12.htm

*Romans 16 NIV.* (2024). Biblehub.com. https://biblehub.com/niv/romans/16.htm

Smith, J. (2021). *The heart of worship: Exploring anointing in modern church settings.* Church Life Publications.

Smith, C., & Snell, P. (2009). *Souls in transition: The religious and spiritual lives of emerging adults.* Oxford University Press.

Stott, J. R. W. (1989). *The message of Ephesians.* InterVarsity Press.

Tozer, A. W. (1990). *Whatever happened to worship?* Christian Publications.

VanGemeren, W. A. (1997). *Interpreting the Old Testament: A guide for exegesis.* Baker Academic.

Wenham, G. J. (2008). *Genesis 16-50.* Word Books.

# ABOUT THE AUTHOR

Dr. Edmond J. Bergeron, a retired U.S. Navy veteran with 20 years of service and over two decades of ministry experience, has served in various roles including pastor, teacher, and leader. He began preaching in 1997 and has since been dedicated to spiritual and practical growth. With a doctorate in education from Liberty University, he combines academic expertise with practical ministry experience.

Printed in the United States
by Baker & Taylor Publisher Services